THE PENGUIN BOOK OF INDIAN RAILWAY STORIES

Ruskin Bond was born in Kasauli, Himachal Pradesh, in 1934, and grew up in Jamnagar (Gujarat), Dehradun and Shimla. In the course of a writing career spanning thirty-five years, he has written over a hundred short stories, essays, novels and more than thirty books for children. Three collections of the short stories, *The Night Train at Deoli Time Stops at Shamli* and *Our Trees Still Grow in Dehra* have been published by Penguin India. He has also edited an anthology, *The Penguin Book of Indian Ghost Stories*.

The Room on the Roof was his first novel, written when he was seventeen, and it received the John Llewellyn Rhys Memorial Prize in 1957. *Vagrants in the Valley* was also written in his teens and picks up from where *The Room on the Roof* leaves off. These two novellas were published in one volume by Penguin India in 1993 as was a much-acclaimed collection of his non-fiction writing, *Rain in the Mountains*.

Ruskin Bond received the Sahitya Akademi Award for English writing in India for 1992, for *Our Trees Still Grow in Dehra*.

ALSO BY RUSKIN BOND

Fiction

The Room on the Roof & Vagrants in the Valley
The Night Train at Deoli and Other Stories
Time Stops at Shamli and Other Stories
Our Trees Still Grow in Dehra
Strangers in the Night: Two Novellas
A Season of Ghosts
When Darkness Falls and Other Stories
A Flight of Pigeons
Delhi Is Not Far
A Face in the Dark and Other Stories

Non-Fiction

Rain in the Mountains
Scenes from a Writer's Life
The Lamp is Lit
The Little Book of Comfort
Landour Days

Anthologies

Collected Fiction (1955–1996)
The Best of Ruskin Bond
Friends in Small Places
Indian Ghost Stories (ed.)
Classic Indian Love Stories and Lyrics (ed.)

The Penguin Book of
INDIAN RAILWAY STORIES

Edited by
Ruskin Bond

PENGUIN BOOKS

PENGUIN BOOKS

USA | Canada | UK | Ireland | Australia
New Zealand | India | South Africa | China

Penguin Books is part of the Penguin Random House group of companies
whose addresses can be found at global.penguinrandomhouse.com

Published by Penguin Random House India Pvt. Ltd
7th Floor, Infinity Tower C, DLF Cyber City,
Gurgaon 122 002, Haryana, India

Penguin
Random House
India

First published by Penguin Books India 1994

ISBN 9780140240665

Typeset in Palatino by FOLIO, New Delhi

Printed at Repro Knowledgecast Limited, India

www.penguin.co.in

FOR ALL MY FAMILY

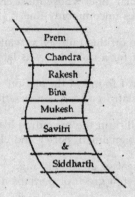

Prem

Chandra

Rakesh

Bina

Mukesh

Savitri

&

Siddharth

Plenty of room on this train!

A Traveller's Tale

There's a North Indian line, whose most cherished design
Is to cut all expenses uncommonly fine.

It once was my fate on this railway to wait
An hour and a half for a train that was late.

The one consolation I found at the station
Was engaging the staff in a long conversation.

And making him shirk in the meantime his work
Of pointsman and signalman, porter and clerk.

He carried a fragment of greasy old rag,
Which had once been a green or perhaps a red flag.

'Why don't they supply a new flag?' said I.
He answered me 'Sahib, *ye-Scotch line to hai.*'

I did not forget, the next time I met
The Agent, to tell him this story, you bet.

He said, when I came to the end of the same,
'I'm thinking ye'll have remembered his name.'

When I said that I had, 'Man,' he said, but I'm glad.
Ram Prasad, was it? Thank you. I'll fine Ram Prasad.

How dare the man wag a dirty old rag
When he knows he's expected to find his own flag?'

A. G. Shirreff
(1917)

Acknowledgements

THE AUTHOR AND PUBLISHERS WOULD like to thank the following for permission to reprint the stories and extracts in this anthology:

Oxford University Press for 'Loyalty' from *Jim Corbett's India* (1952) by Jim Corbett

Ravi Dayal Publishers for the extract from *Train to Pakistan* (1956) by Khushwant Singh. The extract has been titled 'Mano Majra Station' in this anthology

Manoj Das for 'The Intimate Demon' (1985)

Intizar Husain for 'A Stranded Railroad Car' from *The Colour of Nothingness* (Penguin India, 1992)

Sandip Ray for 'Barin Bhowmik's Ailment' from *20 Stories* by Satyajit Ray (Penguin India, 1992)

Bill Aitken for 'Balbir Arora Goes Metric' (1992)

R.K. Laxman for the extract from *The Messenger* by R.K. Laxman (Penguin India, 1993). The extract has been titled 'Railway Reverie' in this anthology

Victor Banerjee for 'Cherry Choo-Choo' (1994)

Manojit Mitra for '99 UP' (1994)

While every effort has been made to trace copyright holders and obtain permission, this has not been possible in all cases; and omissions brought to our attention will be remedied in future editions.

* * *

The editor's special thanks to Rima Handa for her invaluable help in compiling this anthology.

Contents

Soot Gets in Your Eyes

My ANTHOLOGY OF GHOST STORIES for Penguin India, roundly condemned by several critics, almost immediately went into a second edition. And so I feel cocky enough to indulge myself in compiling an anthology on another favourite subject, the Indian railway.

But what is a nature writer doing, putting together a collection of train stories? Who is this upstart Bond, who has been meandering along like a bullock-cart all these years, and now sets himself up as a railway enthusiast? Just what are his credentials?

Few know that my maternal grandfather, William Clerke, was Assistant Station-master at Karachi in the 1920s, or that my uncle, Fred Clark (they spelt their names differently), was Station Superintendent at Delhi Main during World War II. Occasionally, during school holidays, I would stay with Uncle Fred in his bungalow near the station. He had a wind-up gramophone and a large collection of the records of his favourite band, Spike Jones and his City Slickers. This was the noisiest, most irreverent little orchestra in the world, and it deliberately set out to murder any popular tune that took its fancy. Thus, 'Sleepy Lagoon' became 'Sloppy Laggon' and 'Romeo and Juliet' became 'Romeow and Julie-cat'. Uncle Fred liked it because it was the only band that made enough noise to be heard above the shunting of engines, the whistle of passing trains, and the constant clamour from the railway yards. Some of the instruments used by the band had, in fact, been improvised out of scrap metal picked up in locomotive sheds. As music it was horrific, but I was to remain a Spike Jones fan all my life.

The bungalow had a little garden. But the plants and flowers were usually covered with a fine layer of soot from passing steam engines. So much for the romance of railways! No, railway stations and goods yards never were and never will be the haunt of nature lovers.

A few years ago I travelled by a slow passenger train from Dehradun to Bombay: two days and two nights over the dusty plains of Uttar Pradesh, Rajasthan, Madhya Pradesh, Gujarat and Maharashtra. My 'nature notebook' was not idle, and although the proposed essay proved abortive, I kept the rough notes for a piece that was to be called 'Wild Life on a Railway Journey':

1) Myna-bird gets into the compartment at Hardwar and, ticketless, gets out again at Roorkee.
2) Fat, obviously well-fed cockroach lurks in washroom basin.
3) I feed platform dogs and freelance crows with Northern Railway *thali* lunch.
4) Frogs along the west coast—a continuous chanting from the fields as the train rushes by. You can hear them quite clearly above the sound of the train.
5) By the time we reach Bombay, six hours late, washbasin cockroaches have multiplied and look as though they are ready to eat the passengers.

* * *

To be honest, I am not a great railway traveller. I am a poor traveller altogether, being prone to any water-borne infection, unfamiliar food, skin eruptions caused by bugs lurking in the upholstery, suffocation from cigarette and engine smoke, and vertigo from riding in escalators. I am also prone to have things stolen from me. The train stopped at Baroda in the early hours, and a lean hand shot through the window, removing my watch from under my pillow, along with my spectacles, which could have been of no use to anyone, my lens-strength being –7 in one eye and +5 in the other. I had to appear in a Bombay court the next day (having been dragged there to face charges for writing an allegedly obscene short story), and I appeared wearing editor Vinod Mehta's glasses, which were only half the strength of mine. I looked so owlish and helpless that the judge must have felt sorry for me, for the case eventually took a turn in my favour.

But I love railway platforms. I spent a great deal of time on them when I was a boy, waiting for connecting trains to Kalka or Saharanpur or Barrackpore or Rajkot. The odd incident stayed in my memory and when, in my late teens I started writing short stories, those memories became stories such as 'The Night Train at Deoli,' 'The Woman on Platform 8,' 'The Tunnel,' and 'The Eyes Have It.' And when I wasn't sitting on platform benches watching the world and his wife go by, I was browsing at those station bookstalls which were such an institution forty to fifty years ago.

Over a hundred years ago, the Railway booksellers were among the pioneers of publishing in, India.

Take A.H. Wheeler & Co. In the 1880s they started the Indian Railway Library, which saw the first publication of Kipling's early story collections—*Plain Tales from the Hills, Wee Willie Winkle, Under the Deodars, Soldiers Three*—all stories he had written while working for *The Pioneer* of Allahabad or *The Civil and Military Gazette* of Lahore. And what Wheelers was to the north, Higginbothams was to the south.

Kipling was fascinated by the Indian railways, and his in-depth study of the railway headquarters and colony at Jamalpur (E.I. Railway) in *City of Dreadful Night* is a *tour-de-force* of early investigative journalism. It was considered to be rather too long for inclusion here. The railways are ever-present in his fiction, and although some might cavil at 'The Man Who Would Be King' being included in a collection of train stories, that opening scene at Marwar Junction sets the tone and impetus for one of his finest stories. His description of a railway journey in *Kim* is just as relevant today as it was at the turn of the century:

As the 3.25 south-bound roared in, the sleepers sprang

to life, and the station filled with clamour and
shouting, cries of water and sweetmeat vendors,
shouts of policemen, and shrill yells of women
gathering up their baskets, their families, and their
husbands . . . .

Elsewhere he wrote, 'Romance brought up the nine-fifteen,' but
it was really commerce that led to that historic occasion in 1853
when India's first railway train steamed off in an atmosphere
of great excitement from Bombay to Thana, a distance of 34
miles. Within ten years the Great Indian Peninsular Railway
had opened up the cotton-growing areas of the Deccan plateau.
Soon the country was criss-crossed by an extensive network of
railway lines, bringing north to south and east to west, enabling
the mass of Indian people to discover the length, breadth and
diversity of the land for the first time. In pursuing their
commercial interests so effectively, the British rulers had created
unity out of diversity and sown the seeds of nationhood.

Mark Twain, in *A Tramp Abroad*, refers to the 'perennially
ravishing show of Indian railway stations.' There are more than
7,000 of them today, and every one has its own unique
atmosphere. The teeming and varied life of the station and its
environs has fascinated writers from Jules Verne in the 1870s to
Khushwant Singh, Satyajit Ray and other modern writers in
more recent times. Here are stories covering almost every
period of railway history: chosen not because they are history
(which would be to go for dullness) but because they are good
stories or entertaining diversions. Jim Corbett's 'Loyalty' tells
you something about the man himself, his early days with the
railways, and his abiding love for India. 'The Luck of John
Fernandez,' taken from a 1932 issue of the Indian State Railways
Magazine, gives us glimpses into the life of an engine-driver, as
does 'The Bold Prentice'. Unusual encounters on train journeys
are to be found in 'Barin Bhowmik's Ailment' by Satyajit Ray,
'A Stranded Railroad Car' by Intizar Husain and the contribution
of Manoj Das. Intizar Husain is an Urdu writer living in
Pakistan, but as his fine story is set in undivided India it sits
well in this collection. Manoj Das received a Sahitya Akademi
award for his Oriya writing but he is now equally well-known

to English language readers. Bill Aitken makes the grade from Janta class back-pack to the Palace on Wheels. Bill and I were both born in May 1934, in the Year of the Dog, but while Bill became a travelling railway dog, I became a platform dog, although we are both quite good at guard duty. R.K. Laxman, the celebrated cartoonist, gives us a glimpse of his talents as a fiction writer. And the extract from *A Train to Pakistan*, Khushwant Singh's famous novel of the partition of India, tells a powerful and tragic story built around a train journey carrying refugees from the communal holocaust. Manojit Mitra's charming story is about a film star who fails to turn up.

The stories in this collection have been divided into two sections—Stories Before Independence and Stories After Independence. This has been done for the convenience of the observant reader who would be alive to the changing styles, and attitudes of writers from the two periods.

* * *

I started out by saying that nature and the railways had little or no meeting ground. But occasionally there is an exception. As a schoolboy I went to stay with a friend of Uncle Fred's, a station-master at Kalka, where the mountain railway to Simla commences. He had his bungalow on a bare hillside about a mile from the station.

The station-master fancied himself a shikari and always carried his gun around, giving me colourful accounts of his exploits in the jungles. There was no jungle near Kalka, and the only wild animal I saw was a jackal. My host felt he ought to shoot something, if only to demonstrate his skill, and aiming at a crow perched on the compound wall, let off both barrels of his gun and despatched the poor crow half way to the Solan Breweries on the next range.

Minutes later we were being attacked by all the crows in Kalka. About a hundred of them appeared as if from nowhere, and, amidst a deafening cawing, swooped down on us, wings beating furiously. My host's sola-topee was sent flying as he dived for cover. I protected my head with a book I was carrying and ran indoors. We shut ourselves up in the dining-room, while crows gathered at the skylights and windows, pecking on the glass panes. The crows did not give up their siege until late evening when an assistant station-master, accompanied by a fireman, a trolley-driver and several porters came to our rescue. The Night Mail to Delhi was delayed by over an hour, and my host had a nervous breakdown and went on sick leave for a week. As for me, I grew up to have a healthy respect for all crows. They are true survivors and will probably be around long after the human species has disappeared.

* * *

I cannot take leave of the reader without recounting the story of Aunt Mabel and her Persian cat.

Aunt Mabel took her cat wherever she went—to tea parties, bridge parties, hotels, shops and other people's houses, much to everyone's dismay and irritation, for not everyone is a cat-lover, and the Persian variety is inclined to leave a lot of fluff lying around, apart from making forays into kitchens and helping themselves to the fish course. The cat also accompanied Aunt Mabel on long train journeys, but my aunt had an aversion to buying tickets for her pet. She would smuggle the cat into the toilet of her compartment and keep it there whenever we were approaching a station. On one of these journeys, at a whistle-stop somewhere between Bareilly and Lucknow, the cat made her exit from the train via the toilet seat, and was never seen by us again. When we got to Lucknow, Aunt Mabel sent telegrams and wireless messages to all the station masters on the line, but to no avail. The cat had vanished, much to everyone's relief. Aunt Mabel was inconsolable and swore she'd never keep another cat. We told her that this was the right attitude to take. Later we heard that a linesman at Hardoi was the proud owner of a strange-looking cat, and that he fed it on the luddoos that were famous in that region.

Mussoorie   *Ruskin Bond*
January 1994

I

STORIES BEFORE INDEPENDENCE

Around the World in Eighty Days

Jules Verne

This was 1875, and it was the dare of the century!

Phileas Fogg bet his entire fortune that he could cross the 19th century world—with no schedule, no special arrangements, and no air travel—in exactly eighty days. Any delay, any breakdown, and Fogg would lose everything. To complicate matters he is chased by a relentless bounty hunter, Mr Fix, who is convinced Fogg is a fleeing bank robber.

In the following extract Fogg and his companion Passepartout put their trust in the Great Indian Peninsula Railway . . . .

* * *

EVERYBODY KNOWS THAT THE great reversed triangle land, with its base in the north and its apex in the south, which is called India, embraces fourteen hundred thousand square miles, upon which is spread unequally a population of one hundred and eighty millions of souls. The British Crown exercises a real and despotic dominion over the larger portion of this vast country, and has a governor-general stationed at Calcutta, governors at Madras, Bombay, and in Bengal, and a lieutenant-governor at Agra.

But British India, properly so called, only embraces seven hundred thousand square miles, and a population of from one hundred to one hundred and ten millions of inhabitants. A considerable portion of India is still free from British authority; and there are certain ferocious rajahs in the interior who are absolutely independent. The celebrated East India Company was all-powerful from 1756, when the English first gained a foothold on the spot where now stands the city of Madras, down to the time of the great Sepoy insurrection. It gradually annexed province after province, purchasing them of the native chiefs, whom it seldom paid, and appointed the governor-general and his subordinates, civil and military. But the East India Company has now passed away, leaving the British possessions in India directly under the control of the Crown. The aspect of the country, as well as the manners and distinctions of race, is daily changing.

Formerly one was obliged to travel in India by the old cumbrous methods of going on foot or on horseback, in palanquins or unwieldy coaches; now, fast steamboats ply on the Indus and the Ganges, and a great railway, with branch lines joining the main line at many points on its route, traverses the peninsula from Bombay to Calcutta in three days. This railway does not run in a direct line across India. The distance between Bombay and Calcutta, as the bird flies, is only from one thousand to eleven hundred miles; but the deflections of the road increase this distance by more than a third.

The general route of the Great Indian Peninsula Railway is as follows:—Leaving Bombay, it passes through Salcette, crossing to the continent opposite Tannah, goes over the chain of the Western Ghauts, runs thence northeast as far as Burhampoor, skirts the nearly independent territory of Bundelcund, ascends to Allahabad, turns thence eastwardly, meeting the Ganges at Benares, then departs from the river a little, and, descending south-eastward by Burdivan and the French town of Chandernagor, has its terminus at Calcutta.

The passengers of the 'Mongolia' went ashore at half-past four p.m.; at exactly eight the train would start for Calcutta.

Mr Fogg, after bidding good-bye to his whist partners, left the steamer, gave his servant several errands to do, urged it upon him to be at the station promptly at eight, and, with his regular step, which beat to the second, like an astronomical

4

clock, directed his steps to the passport office. As for the wonders of Bombay—its famous city hall, its splendid library, its forts and docks, its bazaars, mosques, synagogues, its Armenian churches, and the noble pagoda on Malebar Hill with its two polygonal towers—he cared not a straw to see them. He would not deign to examine even the masterpieces of Elephanta, or the mysterious hypogea, concealed south-east from the docks, or those fine remains of Buddhist architecture, the Kanherian grottoes of the island of Salcette.

Having transacted his business at the passport office, Phileas Fogg repaired quietly to the railway station, where he ordered dinner. Among the dishes served up to him, the landlord especially recommended a certain giblet of 'native rabbit,' on which he prided himself.

Mr Fogg accordingly tasted the dish, but, despite its spiced sauce, found it far from palatable. He rang for the landlord, and on his appearance, said, fixing his clear eyes upon him, 'Is this rabbit, sir?'

'Yes, my lord,' the rogue boldly replied, 'rabbit from the jungles.'

'And this rabbit did not mew when he was killed?'

'Mew, my lord! what, a rabbit mew! I swear to you—.'

'Be so good, landlord, as not to swear, but remember this: cats were formerly considered, in India, as sacred animals. That was a good time.'

'For the cats, my lord?'

'Perhaps for the travellers as well!'

After which Mr Fogg quietly continued his dinner. Fix had gone on shore shortly after Mr Fogg, and his first destination was the head-quarters of the Bombay police. He made himself known as a London detective, told his business at Bombay, and the position of affairs relative to the supposed robber, and nervously asked if a warrant had arrived from London. It had not reached the office; indeed, there had not yet been time for it to arrive. Fix was sorely disappointed, and tried to obtain an order of arrest from the director of the Bombay police. This the director refused, as the matter concerned the London office, which alone could legally deliver the warrant. Fix did not insist, and was fain to resign himself to await the arrival of the important document; but he was determined not to lose sight of the mysterious rogue as long as he stayed in Bombay. He did not doubt for a moment, any more than Passepartout, that Phileas Fogg would remain there, at least until it was time for the warrant to arrive.

Passepartout, however, had no sooner heard his master's orders on leaving the 'Mongolia,' than he saw at once that they were to leave Bombay as they had done Suez and Paris, and that the journey would be extended at least as far as Calcutta, and perhaps beyond that place. He began to ask himself if this bet that Mr Fogg talked about was not really in good earnest, and whether his fate was not in truth forcing him, despite his love of repose, around the world in eighty days!

Having purchased the usual quota of shirts and shoes, he took a leisurely promenade about the streets, where crowds of people of many nationalities—Europeans, Persians with pointed caps, Banyas with round turbans, Sindes with square bonnets, Parsees with black mitres, and long-robed Armenians—were collected. It happened to be the day of a Parsee festival. These descendants of the sect of Zoroaster—the most thrifty, civilized, intelligent, and austere of the East Indians, among whom are counted the richest native merchants of Bombay—were celebrating a sort of religious carnival, with processions and shows, in the midst of which Indian dancing-girls, clothed in rose-coloured gauze, looped up with gold and silver, danced airily, but with perfect modesty, to the sound of viols and the clanging of tambourines. It is needless to say that Passepartout watched these curious ceremonies with staring eyes and gaping mouth, and that his countenance was that of the greenest booby imaginable.

Unhappily for his master, as well as himself, his curiosity drew him unconsciously farther off than he intended to go. At last, having seen the Parsee carnival wind away in the distance, he was turning his steps towards the station, when he happened to espy the splendid pagoda on Malebar Hill, and was seized with an irresistible desire to see its interior. He was quite ignorant that it is forbidden to Christians to enter certain Indian temples, and that even the faithful must not go in without first leaving their shoes outside the door. It may be said here that the wise policy of the British Government severely punishes a disregard of the practices of the native religions.

Passepartout, however, thinking no harm, went in like a simple tourist, and was soon lost in admiration of the splendid Brahmin ornamentation which everywhere met his eyes, when of a sudden he found himself sprawling on the sacred flagging. He looked up to behold three enraged priests, who forthwith fell upon him, tore off his shoes, and began to beat him with loud, savage exclamations. The agile Frenchman was soon upon his feet again, and lost no time in knocking down two of his long-gowned adversaries with his fists and a vigorous application of his toes; then, rushing out of the pagoda as fast as his legs could carry him, he soon escaped the third priest by mingling with the crowd in the streets.

At five minutes before eight, Passepartout, hatless, shoeless, and having in the squabble lost his package of shirts and shoes, rushed breathlessly into the station.

Fix, who had followed Mr Fogg to the station, and saw that he was really going to leave Bombay, was there, upon the platform. He had resolved to follow the supposed robber to Calcutta, and farther, if necessary. Passepartout did not observe the detective, who stood in an obscure corner; but Fix heard him relate his adventures in a few words to Mr Fogg.

'I hope that this will not happen again,' said Phileas Fogg, coldly, as he got into the train. Poor Passepartout, quite crestfallen, followed his master without a word. Fix was on the point of entering another carriage, when an idea struck him which induced him to alter his plan.

'No, I'll stay,' muttered he. 'An offence has been committed on Indian soil. I've got my man.'

Just then the locomotive gave a sharp screech, and the train passed out into the darkness of the night.

* * *

The train had started punctually. Among the passengers were a number of officers, Government officials, and opium and indigo merchants, whose business called them to the eastern coast. Passepartout rode in the same carriage with his master, and a third passenger occupied a seat opposite to them. This was Sir Francis Cromarty, one of Mr Fogg's whist partners on the 'Mongolia,' now on his way to join his corps at Benares. Sir Francis was a tall, fair man of fifty, who had greatly distinguished himself in the last Sepoy revolt. He made India his home, only paying brief visits to England at rare intervals; and was almost as familiar as a native with the customs, history, and character of India and its people. But Phileas Fogg, who was not travelling, but only describing a circumference, took no pains to inquire into these subjects; he was a solid body, traversing an orbit around the terrestrial globe, according to the laws of rational mechanics. He was at this moment calculating in his mind the number of hours spent since his departure from London, and, had it been in his nature to make a useless demonstration, would have rubbed his hands for satisfaction. Sir Francis Cromarty had observed the oddity of his travelling companion—although the only opportunity he had for studying him had been while he was dealing the cards, and between two rubbers—and questioned himself whether a human heart really beat beneath this cold exterior, and whether Phileas Fogg had any sense of the beauties of nature. The brigadier-general was free to mentally confess, that, of all the eccentric persons he had ever met, none was comparable to this product of the exact sciences.

Phileas Fogg had not concealed from Sir Francis his design of going round the world, nor the circumstances under which he set out; and the general only saw in the wager a useless eccentricity, and a lack of sound commonsense. In the way this strange gentleman was going on, he would leave the world without having done any good to himself or anybody else.

An hour after leaving Bombay the train had passed the viaducts and the island of Salcette, and had got into the open country. At Callyan they reached the junction of the branch line which descends towards south-eastern India by Kandallah and Pounah; and, passing Pauwell, they entered the defiles of the mountains, with their basalt bases, and their summits crowned with thick and verdant forests. Phileas Fogg and Sir Francis Cromarty exchanged a few words from time to time, and now Sir Francis, reviving the conversation, observed, 'Some years ago, Mr Fogg, you would have met with a delay at this point, which would probably have lost you your wager.'

'How so, Sir Francis?'

'Because the railway stopped at the base of these mountains, which the passengers were obliged to cross in palanquins or on ponies to Kandallah, on the other side.'

'Such a delay would not have deranged my plans in the least,' said Mr Fogg. 'I have constantly foreseen the likelihood of certain obstacles.'

'But, Mr Fogg,' pursued Sir Francis, 'you run the risk of having some difficulty about this worthy fellow's adventure at the pagoda.' Passepartout, his feet comfortably wrapped in his travelling-blanket, was sound asleep, and did not dream that anybody was talking about him. 'The Government is very severe upon that kind of offence. It takes particular care that the religious customs of the Indians should be respected, and if your servant were caught—.'

'Very well, Sir Francis,' replied Mr Fogg; 'if he had been caught he would have been condemned and punished, and then would have quietly returned to Europe. I don't see how this affair could have delayed his master.'

The conversation fell again. During the night the train left the mountains behind, and passed Nassik, and the next day proceeded over the flat, well-cultivated country of the Khandeish, with its straggling villages, above which rose the minarets of the pagodas. This fertile territory is watered by numerous small rivers and limpid streams, mostly tributaries of the Godavery.

Passepartout, on waking and looking out, could not realize that he was actually crossing India in a railway train. The locomotive, guided by an English engineer and fed with English coal, threw out its smoke upon cotton, coffee, nutmeg, clove, and pepper plantations, while the steam curled in spirals around groups of palm-trees, in the midst of which were seen picturesque bungalows, viharis (a sort of abandoned monasteries), and marvellous temples enriched by the exhaustless ornamentation of Indian architecture. Then they came upon vast tracts extending to the horizon, with jungles inhabited by snakes and tigers, which fled at the noise of the train; succeeded by forests penetrated by the railway, and still haunted by elephants which, with pensive eyes, gazed at the train as it passed. The travellers crossed, beyond Malligaum, the fatal country so often stained with blood by the sectaries of the goddess Kali. Not far off rose Ellora, with its graceful pagodas, and the famous Aurungabad capital of the ferocious Aureng-Zeb, now the chief town of one of the detached provinces of the kingdom of the Nizam. It was thereabouts that Feringhea, the Thuggee chief, king of the stranglers, held his sway. These ruffians, united by a secret bond, strangled victims of every age in honour of the goddess Death, without ever shedding blood; there was a period when this part of the country could scarcely be travelled over without corpses being found in every direction. The English Government has succeeded in greatly diminishing these murders, though the Thuggees still exist, and pursue the exercise of their horrible rites.

At half-past twelve the train stopped at Burhampoor, where Passepartout was able to purchase some Indian slippers, ornamented with false pearls, in which, with evident vanity, he proceeded to incase his feet. The travellers made a hasty breakfast, and started off for Assurghur, after skirting for a little the banks of the small river Tapty, which empties into the Gulf of Cambray, near Surat.

Passepartout was now plunged into absorbing reverie. Up to his arrival at Bombay, he had entertained hopes that their journey would end there; but now that they were plainly whirling across India at full speed, a sudden change had come over the spirit of his dreams. His old vagabond nature returned to him; the fantastic ideas of his youth once more took possession of him. He came to regard his master's project as intended in good earnest, believed in the reality of the bet, and therefore in the tour of the world, and the necessity of making it without fail within the designated period. Already he began to worry about possible delays, and accidents which might happen on the way. He recognized himself as being personally interested in the wager, and trembled at the thought that he might have been the means of losing it by his unpardonable folly of the night before. Being much less cool-headed than Mr Fogg, he was much more restless, counting and recounting the days passed over, uttering maledictions when the train stopped, and accusing it of sluggishness, and mentally blaming Mr Fogg for not having bribed the engineer. The worthy fellow was ignorant that, while it was possible by such means to hasten the rate of a steamer, it could not be done on the railway.

The train entered the defiles of the Sutpour Mountains, which separate the Khandeish from Bundelcund, towards evening. The next day Sir Francis Cromarty asked Passepartout what time it was; to which, on consulting his watch, he replied that it was three in the morning. This famous timepiece, always regulated on the Greenwich meridian, which was now some seventy-seven degrees westward, was at least four hours slow. Sir Francis corrected Passepartout's time, whereupon the latter made the same remark that he had done to Fix; and upon the general insisting that the watch should be regulated in each new meridian, since he was constantly going eastward, that is in the face of the sun, and therefore the days were shorter by four minutes for each degree gone over, Passepartout obstinately refused to alter his watch, which he kept at London time. It was an innocent delusion which could harm no one.

The train stopped, at eight o'clock, in the midst of a glade some fifteen miles beyond Rothal, where there were several bungalows and workmen's cabins. The conductor, passing along the carriages, shouted, 'Passengers will get out here!'

Phileas Fogg looked at Sir Francis Cromarty for an explanation; but the general could not tell what meant a halt in the midst of this forest of dates and acacias.

Passepartout, not less surprised, rushed out and speedily returned, crying, 'Monsieur, no more railway!'

'What do you mean?' asked Sir Francis.

'I mean to say that the train isn't going on.'

The general at once stepped out, while Phileas Fogg calmly followed him, and they proceeded together to the conductor.

'Where are we?' asked Sir Francis.

'At the hamlet of Kholby.'

'Do we stop here?'

'Certainly. The railway isn't finished.'

'What! Not finished?'

'No. There's still a matter of fifty miles to be laid from here to Allahabad, where the line begins again.'

11

'But the papers announced the opening of the railway throughout.'

'What would you have, officer? The papers were mistaken.'

'Yet you sell tickets from Bombay to Calcutta,' retorted Sir Francis, who was growing warm.

'No doubt,' replied the conductor; 'but the passengers know that they must provide means of transportation for themselves from Kholby to Allahabad.'

Sir Francis was furious. Passepartout would willingly have knocked the conductor down, and did not dare to look at his master.

'Sir Francis,' said Mr Fogg, quietly, 'we will, if you please, look about for some means of conveyance to Allahabad.'

'Mr Fogg, this is a delay greatly to your disadvantage.'

'No, Sir Francis; it was foreseen.'

'What! You knew that the way—.'

'Not at all; but I knew that some obstacle or other would sooner or later arise on my route. Nothing, therefore, is lost. I have two days which I have already gained to sacrifice. A steamer leaves Calcutta for Hong Kong at noon, on the 25th. This is the 22nd, and we shall reach Calcutta in time.'

There was nothing to say to so confident a response.

It was but too true that the railway came to a termination at this point. The papers were like some watches, which have a way of getting too fast, and had been premature in their announcement of the completion of the line. The greater part of the travellers were aware of this interruption, and leaving the train, they began to engage such vehicles as the village could provide—four-wheeled palkigharis, waggons drawn by zebus, carriages that looked like perambulating pagodas, palanquins, ponies, and what not.

Mr Fogg and Sir Francis Cromarty, after searching the village from end to end, came back without having found anything.

'I shall go afoot,' said Phileas Fogg.

Passepartout, who had now rejoined his master, made a wry grimace, as he thought of his magnificent, but too frail Indian shoes. Happily he too had been looking about him, and, after a moment's hesitation, said, 'Monsieur, I think I have found a means of conveyance.'

'What?'

'An elephant! An elephant that belongs to an Indian who lives but a hundred steps from here.'

'Let's go and see the elephant,' replied Mr Fogg.

They soon reached a small hut, near which, enclosed within some high pailings, was the animal in question. An Indian came out of the hut, and, at their request, conducted them within the enclosure. The elephant, which its owner had reared, not for a beast of burden, but for warlike purposes, was half domesticated. The Indian had begun already, by often irritating him, and feeding him every three months on sugar and butter, to impart to him a ferocity not in his nature, this method being often employed by those who train the Indian elephants for battle. Happily, however, for Mr Fogg, the animal's instruction in this direction had not gone far, and the elephant still preserved his natural gentleness. Kiouni—this was the name of the beast—could doubtless travel rapidly for a long time, and, in default of any other means of conveyance, Mr Fogg resolved to hire him. But elephants are far from cheap in India, where they are becoming scarce; the males, which alone are suitable for circus shows, are much sought, especially as but few of them are domesticated. When, therefore, Mr Fogg proposed to the Indian to hire Kiouni, he refused point-blank. Mr Fogg persisted, offering the excessive sum of ten pounds an hour for the loan of the beast to Allahabad. Refused. Twenty pounds? Refused also. Forty pounds? Still refused. Passepartout jumped at each advance; but the Indian declined to be tempted. Yet the offer was an alluring one, for, supposing it took the elephant fifteen hours to reach Allahabad, his owner would receive no less than six hundred pounds sterling.

Phileas Fogg, without getting in the least flurried, then proposed to purchase the animal outright, and at first offered a thousand pounds for him. The Indian, perhaps thinking he was going to make a great bargain, still refused.

Sir Francis Cromarty took Mr Fogg aside, and begged him to reflect before he went any further; to which that gentleman replied that he was not in the habit of acting rashly, that a bet

13

of twenty thousand pounds was at stake, that the elephant was absolutely necessary to him, and that he would secure him if he had to pay twenty times his value. Returning to the Indian, whose sharp eyes betrayed that with him it was only a question of how great a price he could obtain, Mr Fogg offered first twelve hundred, then fifteen hundred, eighteen hundred, two thousand pounds. Passepartout, usually so rubicund, was fairly white with suspense.

At two thousand pounds the Indian yielded.

'What a price, good heaven!' cried Passepartout, 'for an elephant!'

It only remained now to find a guide, which was comparatively easy. A young Parsee, with an intelligent face, offered his services, which Mr Fogg accepted, promising so generous a reward as to materially stimulate his zeal. The elephant was led out and equipped. The Parsee, who was an accomplished elephant driver, covered his back with a sort of saddle-cloth, and attached to each of his flanks some curiously uncomfortable howdahs.

* * *

Fogg and his companions continue their journey through the Indian forests.

The Man Who Would Be King

Rudyard Kipling

'BROTHER TO A PRINCE AND fellow to a beggar if he be found worthy.'

The Law, as quoted, lays down a fair conduct of life, and one not easy to follow. I have been fellow to a beggar again and again under circumstances which prevented either of us finding out whether the other was worthy. I have still to be brother to a Prince, though I once came near to kinship with what might have been a veritable King and was promised the reversion of a Kingdom—army, law-courts, revenue and policy all complete. But, to-day, I greatly fear that my King is dead, and if I want a crown I must go and hunt it for myself.

The beginning of everything was in a railway train upon the road to Mhow from Ajmir. There had been a Deficit in the Budget, which necessitated travelling, not Second-class, which is only half as dear as First-class, but by Intermediate, which is very awful indeed. There are no cushions in the Intermediate class, and the population are either Intermediate, which is Eurasian, or native, which for a long night journey is nasty, or Loafer, which is amusing though intoxicated. Intermediates do not patronize refreshment-rooms. They carry their food in bundles and pots, and buy sweets from the native sweet-meat-sellers, and drink the roadside water. That is why in the hot weather Intermediates are taken out of the carriages dead, and in all weathers are most properly looked down upon.

My particular Intermediate happened to be empty till I reached Nasirabad, when a huge gentleman in shirt-sleeves entered, and, following the custom of Intermediates, passed the time of day. He was a wanderer and a vagabond like myself, but with an educated taste for whisky. He told tales of things he had seen and done, of out-of-the-way corners of the Empire into which he had penetrated, and of adventures in which he risked his life for a few days' food. 'If India was filled with men like you and me, not knowing more than the crows where they'd get their next day's rations, it isn't seventy millions of revenue the land would be paying—it's seven hundred millions,' said he; and as I looked at his mouth and chin I was disposed to agree with him. We talked politics—the politics of Loaferdom that sees things from the underside where the lath and plaster is not smoothed off—and we talked postal arrangements because my friend wanted to send a telegram back from the next station to Ajmir, which is the turning-off place from the Bombay to the Mhow line as you travel westward. My friend had no money beyond eight annas which he wanted for dinner, and I had no money at all, owing to the hitch in the Budget before mentioned. Further, I was going into a wilderness where, though I should resume touch with the Treasury, there were no telegraph offices. I was, therefore, unable to help him in any way.

'We might threaten a Station-master, and make him send a wire on tick,' said my friend, 'but that'd mean inquiries for you and for me, and I've got my hands full these days. Did you say you are travelling back along this line within any days?'

'Within ten,' I said.

'Can't you make it eight?' said he. 'Mine is rather urgent business.'

'I can send your telegram within ten days if that will serve you,' I said.

'I couldn't trust the wire to fetch him now I think of it. It's this way. He leaves Delhi on the 23d for Bombay. That means he'll be running through Ajmir about the night of the 23d.'

'But I am going into the Indian Desert,' I explained.

'Well *and* good,' said he. 'You'll be changing at Marwar Junction to get into Jodhpore territory—you must do that— and he'll be coming through Marwar Junction in the early

16

morning of the 24th by the Bombay Mail. Can you be at Marwar Junction on that time? 'Twon't be inconveniencing you because I know that there's precious few pickings to be got out of these Central India States—even though you pretend to be correspondent of the *Backwoodsman*.'

'Have you ever tried that trick?' I asked.

'Again and again, but the Residents find you out, and then you get escorted to the Border before you've time to get your knife into them. But about my friend here. I *must* give him a word o'mouth to tell him what's come to me or else he won't know where to go. I would take it more than kind of you if you was to come out of Central India in time to catch him at Marwar Junction, and say to him:—'He has gone South for the week.' He'll know what that means. He's a big man with a red beard, and a great swell he is. You'll find him sleeping like a gentleman with all his luggage round him in a Second-class compartment. But don't you be afraid. Slip down the window, and say:—'He has gone South for the week,' and he'll tumble. It's only cutting your time of stay in those parts by two days. I ask you as a stranger—going to the West,' he said, with emphasis.

'Where have *you* come from?' said I.

'From the East,' said he, 'and I am hoping that you will give him the message on the Square—for the sake of my Mother as well as your own.'

Englishmen are not usually softened by appeals to the memory of their mothers, but for certain reasons, which will be fully apparent, I saw fit to agree.

'It's more than a little matter,' said he, 'and that's why I ask you to do it—and now I know that I can depend on you doing it. A Second-class carriage at Marwar Junction, and a red-haired man asleep in it. You'll be sure to remember. I get out at the next station, and I must hold on there till he comes or sends me what I want.'

'I'll give the message if I catch him,' I said, 'and for the sake of your Mother as well as mine I'll give you a word of advice. Don't try to run the Central India States just now as the correspondent of the *Backwoodsman*. There's a real one knocking about here, and it might lead to trouble.'

17

'Thank you,' said he, simply, 'and when will the swine be gone? I can't starve because he's ruining my work. I wanted to get hold of the Degumber Rajah down here about his father's widow, and give him a jump.'

'What did he do to his father's widow, then?'

'Filled her up with red pepper and slippered her to death as she hung from a beam. I found that out myself and I'm the only man that would dare going into the State to get hush-money for it. They'll try to poison me, same as they did in Chortumna when I went on the loot there. But you'll give the man at Marwar Junction my message?'

He got out at a little roadside station, and I reflected. I had heard, more than once, of men personating correspondents of newspapers and bleeding small Native States with threats of exposure, but I had never met any of the caste before. They lead a hard life, and generally die with great suddenness. The Native States have a wholesome horror of English newspapers, which may throw light on their peculiar methods of government, and do their best to choke correspondence with champagne, or drive them out of their mind with four-in-hand barouches. They do not understand that nobody cares a straw for the internal administration of Native States so long as oppression and crime are kept within decent limits, and the ruler is not drugged, drunk, or diseased from one end of the year to the other. Native States were created by Providence in order to supply picturesque scenery, tigers, and tall-writing. They are the dark places of the earth, full of unimaginable cruelty, touching the Railway and the Telegraph on one side, and, on the other, the days of Harun-al-Raschid. When I left the train I did business with divers Kings, and in eight days passed through many changes of life. Sometimes I wore dress-clothes and consorted with Princes and Politicals, drinking from crystal and eating from silver. Sometimes I lay out upon the ground and devoured what I could get, from a plate made of a flapjack, and drank the running water, and slept under the same rug as my servant. It was all in the day's work.

Then I headed for the Great Indian Desert upon the proper date, as I had promised, and the night Mail set me down at Marwar Junction, where a funny little, happy-go-lucky, native-managed railway runs to Jodhpore. The Bombay Mail from Delhi makes a short halt at Marwar. She arrived as I got in, and I had just time to hurry to her platform and go down the carriages. There was only one Second-class on the train. I slipped the window and looked down upon a flaming red beard, half covered by a railway rug. That was my man, fast asleep, and I dug him gently in the ribs. He woke with a grunt and I saw his face in the light of the lamps. It was a great and shining face.

'Tickets again?' said he.

'No,' said I. 'I am to tell you that he is gone South for the week. He is gone South for the week!'

The train had begun to move out. The red man rubbed his eyes. 'He has gone South for the week,' he repeated. 'Now that's just like his impidence. Did he say that I was to give you anything?—'Cause I won't.'

'He didn't,' I said, and dropped away, and watched the red lights die out in the dark. It was horribly cold because the wind was blowing off the sands. I climbed into my own train—not an Intermediate Carriage this time—and went to sleep.

If the man with the beard had given me a rupee I should have kept it as a memento of a rather curious affair. But the consciousness of having done my duty was my only reward.

Later on I reflected that two gentlemen like my friends could not do any good if they foregathered and personated correspondents of newspapers, and might, if they 'stuck up' one of the little rat-trap states of Central India or Southern Rajputana, get themselves into serious difficulties. I therefore took some trouble to describe them as accurately as I could remember to people who would be interested in deporting them: and succeeded, so I was later informed, in having them headed back from the Degumber border.

Then I became respectable, and returned to an Office where there were no Kings and no incidents except the daily manufacture of a newspaper. A newspaper office seems to attract every conceivable sort of person, to the prejudice of discipline. Zenana-mission ladies arrive, and beg that the Editor will instantly abandon all his duties to describe a Christian prize-giving in a back-slum of a perfectly inaccessible village; Colonels who have been overpassed for commands sit down

19

and sketch the outline of a series of ten, twelve, or twenty-four leading articles on Seniority *versus* Selection; missionaries wish to know why they have not been permitted to escape from their regular vehicles of abuse and swear at a brother-missionary under special patronage of the editorial We; stranded theatrical companies troop up to explain that they cannot pay for their advertisements, but on their return from New Zealand or Tahiti will do so with interest; inventors of patent punkah-pulling machines, carriage couplings and unbreakable swords and axle-trees call with specifications in their pockets and hours at their disposal; tea-companies enter and elaborate their prospectuses with the office pens; secretaries of ball-committees clamour to have the glories of their last dance more fully expounded; strange ladies rustle in and say:—'I want a hundred lady's cards printed *at once*, please,' which is manifestly part of an Editor's duty; and every dissolute ruffian that ever tramped the Grand Trunk Road makes it his business to ask for employment as a proof-reader. And, all the time, the telephone-bell is ringing madly, and Kings are being killed on the Continent, and Empires are saying—'You're another,' and Mister Gladstone is calling down brimstone upon the British Dominions, and the little black copy-boys are whining, *'kaa-pi chay-ha-yeh'* (copy wanted) like tired bees, and most of the paper is as blank as Modred's shield.

But that is the amusing part of the year. There are other six months wherein none ever come to call, and the thermometer walks inch by inch up to the top of the glass, and the office is darkened to just above reading-light, and the press machines are red-hot of touch, and nobody writes anything but accounts of amusements in the Hill-stations or obituary notices. Then the telephone becomes a thinking terror, because it tells you of the sudden deaths of men and women that you knew intimately, and the prickly-heat covers you as with a garment, and you sit down and write:—'A slight increase of sickness is reported from the Khuda Janta Khan District. The outbreak is purely sporadic in its nature, and, thanks to the energetic efforts of the District authorities, is now almost at an end. It is, however, with deep regret we record the death, etc.'

Then the sickness really breaks out, and the less recording

and reporting the better for the peace of the subscribers. But the Empires and the Kings continue to divert themselves as selfishly as before, and the Foreman thinks that a daily paper really ought to come out once in twenty-four hours, and all the people at the Hill-stations in the middle of their amusements say:—'Good gracious! Why can't the paper be sparkling? I'm sure there's plenty going on up here.'

That is the dark half of the moon, and, as the advertisements say, 'must be experienced to be appreciated.'

It was in that season, and a remarkably evil season, that the paper began running the last issue of the week on Saturday night, which is to say Sunday morning, after the custom of a London paper. This was a great convenience, for immediately after the paper was put to bed, the dawn would lower the thermometer from 96° to almost 84° for half an hour, and in that chill—you have no idea how cold is 84° on the grass until you begin to pray for it—a very tired man could set off to sleep ere the heat roused him.

One Saturday night it was my pleasant duty to put the paper to bed alone. A King or courtier or a courtesan or a community was going to die or get a new Constitution, or do something that was important on the other side of the world, and the paper was to be held open till the latest possible minute in order to catch the telegram. It was a pitchy black night, as stifling as a June night can be, and the *loo*, the red-hot wind from the westward, was booming among the tinder-dry trees and pretending that the rain was on its heels. Now and again a spot of almost boiling water would fall on the dust with the flop of a frog, but all our weary world knew that was only pretence. It was a shade cooler in the press-room than the office, so I sat there, while the type ticked and clicked, and the night-jars hooted at the windows, and the all but naked compositors wiped the sweat from their foreheads and called for water. The thing that was keeping us back, whatever it was, would not come off, though the *loo* dropped and the last type was set, and the whole round earth stood still in the choking heat, with its finger on its lip, to wait the event. I drowsed, and wondered whether the telegraph was a blessing, and whether this dying man, or struggling people, was aware of the

21

inconvenience the delay was causing. There was no special reason beyond the heat and worry to make tension, but, as the clock hands crept up to three o'clock and the machines spun their flywheels two and three times to see that all was in order, before I said the word that would set them off, I could have shrieked aloud.

Then the roar and rattle of the wheels shivered the quiet into little bits. I rose to go away, but two men in white clothes stood in front of me. The first one said:—'It's him!' The second said:—'So it is!' And they both laughed almost as loudly as the machinery roared, and mopped their foreheads. 'We see there was a light burning across the road and we were sleeping in that ditch there for coolness, and I said to my friend here, The office is open. Let's come along and speak to him as turned us back from the Degumber State,' said the smaller of the two. He was the man I had met in the Mhow train, and his fellow was the red-bearded man of Marwar Junction. There was no mistaking the eyebrows of the one or the beard of the other.

I was not pleased, because I wished to go to sleep, not to squabble with loafers. 'What do you want?' I asked.

'Half an hour's talk with you cool and comfortable, in the office,' said the red-bearded man. 'We'd *like* some drink—the Contrack doesn't begin yet, Peachey, so you needn't look—but what we really want is advice. We don't want money. We ask you as a favour, because you did us a bad turn about Degumber.'

I led from the press-room to the stifling office with the maps on the walls, and the red-haired man rubbed his hands. 'That's something like,' said he. 'This was the proper shop to come to. Now, Sir, let me introduce to you Brother Peachey Carnehan, that's him, and Brother Daniel Dravot, that is *me*, and the less said about our professions the better, for we have been most things in our time. Soldier, sailor, compositor, photographer, proof-reader, street-preacher, and correspondents of the *Backwoodsman* when we thought the paper wanted one. Carnehan is sober, and so am I. Look at us first and see that's sure. It will save you cutting into my talk. We'll take one of your cigars apiece, and you shall see us light.'

I watched the test. The men were absolutely sober so I gave them each a tepid peg.

22

'Well *and* good,' said Carnehan of the eyebrows, wiping the froth from his moustache. 'Let me talk now, Dan. We have been all over India, mostly on foot. We have been boiler-fitters, engine-drivers, petty contractors, and all that, and we have decided that India isn't big enough for such as us.'

They certainly were too big for the office. Dravot's beard seemed to fill half the room and Carnehan's shoulders the other half, as they sat on the big table. Carnehan continued:— 'The country isn't half worked out because they that governs it won't let you touch it. They spend all their blessed time in governing it, and you can't lift a spade, nor chip a rock, nor look for oil, nor anything like that without all the Government saying—"Leave it alone and let us govern." Therefore, such as it is, we will let it alone, and go away to some other place where a man isn't crowded and can come to his own. We are not little men, and there is nothing that we are afraid of except Drink, and we have signed a Contrack on that. *Therefore*, we are going away to be Kings.'

'Kings in our own right,' muttered Dravot.

'Yes, of course,' I said. 'You've been tramping in the sun, and it's a very warm night, and hadn't you better sleep over the notion? Come tomorrow.'

'Neither drunk nor sunstruck,' said Dravot. 'We have slept over the notion half a year, and require to see Books and Atlases, and we have decided that there is only one place now in the world that two strong men can Sar-a-*whack*. They call it Kafiristan. By my reckoning it's the top right-hand corner of Afghanistan, not more than three hundred miles from Peshawur. They have two and thirty heathen idols there, and we'll be the thirty-third. It's a mountaineous country, and the women of those parts are very beautiful.'

'But that is provided against in the Contrack,' said Carnehan. 'Neither Women nor Liqu-or, Daniel.'

'And that's all we know, except that no one has gone there, and they fight, and in any place where they fight a man who knows how to drill men can always be a King. We shall go to those parts and say to any King we find—"D'you want to vanquish your foes?" and we will show him how to drill men; for that we know better than anything else. Then we

23

will subvert that King and seize his Throne and establish a Dynasty.'

'You'll be cut to pieces before you're fifty miles across the Border,' I said. 'You have to travel through Afghanistan to get to that country. It's one mass of mountains and peaks and glaciers, and no Englishman has been through it. The people are utter brutes, and even if you reached them you couldn't do anything.'

'That's more like,' said Carnehan. 'If you could think us a little more mad we would be more pleased. We have come to you to know about this country, to read a book about it, and to be shown maps. We want you to tell us that we are fools and to show us your books.' He turned to the bookcases.

'Are you at all in earnest?' I said.

'A little,' said Dravot, sweetly. 'As big a map as you have got, even if it's all blank where Kafiristan is, and any books you've got. We can read, though we aren't very educated.'

I uncased the big thirty-two-miles-to-the-inch-map of India, and two smaller Frontier maps, hauled down volume INFKAN of the *Encyclopædia Britannica*, and the men consulted them.

'See here!' said Dravot, his thumb on the map. 'Up to Jagdallak, Peachey and me know the road. We was there with Roberts's Army. We'll have to turn off to the right at Jagdallak through Laghmann territory. Then we get among the hills— fourteen thousand feet—fifteen thousand—it will be cold work there, but it don't look very far on the map.'

I handed him Wood on the *Sources of the Oxus*. Carnehan was deep in the *Encyclopædia*.

'They're a mixed lot,' said Dravot, reflectively; 'and it won't help us to know the names of their tribes. The more tribes the more they'll fight, and the better for us. From Jagdallak to Ashang. H'mm!'

'But all the information about the country is as sketchy and inaccurate as can be,' I protested. 'No one knows anything about it really. Here's the file of the *United Services' Institute*. Read what Bellew says.'

'Blow Bellew!' said Carnehan. 'Dan they're an all-fired lot of heathens, but this book here says they think they're related to us English.'

I smoked while the men pored over *Raverty*, *Wood*, the maps and the *Encyclopædia*.

'There is no use your waiting,' said Dravot, politely. 'It's about four o'clock now. We'll go before six o'clock if you want to sleep, and we won't steal any of the papers. Don't you sit up. We're two harmless lunatics, and if you come, to-morrow evening, down to the Serai we'll say good-bye to you.'

'You *are* two fools,' I answered. 'You'll be turned back at the Frontier or cut up the minute you set foot in Afghanistan. Do you want any money or a recommendation down-country? I can help you to the chance of work next week.'

'Next week we shall be hard at work ourselves, thank you,' said Dravot. 'It isn't so easy being a King as it looks. When we've got our Kingdom in going order we'll let you know, and you can come up and help us to govern it.'

'Would two lunatics make a Contrack like that?' said Carnehan, with subdued pride, showing me a greasy half-sheet of note-paper on which was written the following. I copied it, then and there, as a curiosity:

This Contract between me and you persuing witnesseth in the name of God—Amen and so forth.

(One) That me and you will settle this matter together: i.e., to be Kings of Kafiristan.

(Two) That you and me will not, while this matter is being settled, look at any Liquor, nor any Woman, black, white or brown, so as to get mixed up with one or the other harmful.

(Three) That we conduct ourselves with dignity and discretion, and if one of us gets into trouble the other will stay by him.

Signed by you and me this day.

Peachey Taliaferro Carnehan.

Daniel Dravot.

Both Gentlemen at Large.

'There was no need for the last article,' said Carnehan, blushing modestly; 'But it looks regular. Now you know the sort of men that loafers are—we *are* loafers, Dan, until we get out of India—

25

and *do* you think that we would sign a Contrack like that unless we was in earnest? We have kept away from the two things that make life worth having.'

'You won't enjoy your lives much longer if you are going to try this idiotic adventure. Don't set the office on fire,' I said, 'and go away before nine o'clock.'

I left them still poring over the maps and making notes on the back of the 'Contrack.' 'Be sure to come down to the Serai to-morrow,' were their parting words.

The Kumharsen Serai is the great four-square sink of humanity where the strings of camels and horses from the North load and unload. All the nationalities of Central Asia may be found there, and most of the folk of India proper. Balkh and Bokhara there meet Bengal and Bombay and try to draw eye-teeth. You can buy ponies, turquoises, Persian pussy-cats, saddle-bags, fat-tailed sheep and musk in the Kumharsen Serai, and get many strange things for nothing. In the afternoon I went down there to see whether my friends intended to keep their word or were lying about drunk.

A priest attired in fragments of ribbons and rags stalked up to me, gravely twisting a child's paper whirligig. Behind him was his servant bending under the load of a crate of mud toys. The two were loading up two camels, and the inhabitants of the Serai watched them with shrieks of laughter.

'The priest is mad,' said a horse-dealer to me. 'He is going up to Kabul to sell toys to the Amir. He will either be raised to honour or have his head cut off. He came in here this morning and has been behaving madly ever since.'

'The witless are under the protection of God,' stammered a flat-cheeked Usbeg in broken Hindi. 'They foretell future events.'

'Would they could have foretold that my caravan would have been cut up by the Shinwaris almost within shadow of the Pass!' grunted the Eusufzai agent of a Rajputana trading-house whose goods had been feloniously diverted into the hands of other robbers just across the Border, and whose misfortunes were the laughing-stock of the bazaar. 'Ohé, priest, whence come you and whither do you go?'

'From Roum have I come,' shouted the priest, waving his whirligig; 'from Roum, blown by the breath of a hundred

devils across the sea! O thieves, robbers, liars, the blessing of
Pir Khan on pigs, dogs, and perjurers! Who will take the
Protected of God to the North to sell charms that are never still
to the Amir? The camels shall not gall, the sons shall not fall
sick, and the wives shall remain faithful while they are away,
of the men who give me place in their caravan. Who will assist
me to slipper the King of the Roos with a golden slipper with
a silver heel? The protection of Pir Khan be upon his labours!'
He spread out the skirts of his gaberdine and pirouetted between
the lines of tethered horses.

'There starts a caravan from Peshawur to Kabul in twenty
days, *Huzrut,'* said the Eusufzai trader. 'My camels go therewith.
Do thou also go and bring us good-luck.'

'I will go even now!' shouted the priest. 'I will depart upon
my winged camels, and be at Peshawur in a day! Ho! Hazar
Mir Khan,' he yelled to his servant, 'drive out the camels, but
let me first mount my own.'

He leaped on the back of his beast as it knelt, and, turning
round to me, cried:—'Come thou also, Sahib, a little along the
road and I will sell thee a charm—an amulet that shall make
thee King of Kafiristan.'

Then the light broke upon me and I followed the two
camels out of the Serai till we reached open road and the priest
halted.

'What d' you think o' that?' said he in English. 'Carnehan
can't talk their patter, so I've made him my servant. He makes
a handsome servant. 'Tisn't for nothing that I've been knocking
about the country for fourteen years. Didn't I do that talk neat?
We'll hitch on to a caravan at Peshawur till we get to Jagdallak,
and then we'll see if we can get donkeys for our camels, and
strike into Kafiristan. Whirligigs for the Amir, O Lor! Put your
hand under the camel-bags and tell me what you feel.'

I felt the butt of a Martini, and another and another.

'Twenty of 'em,' said Dravot, placidly. 'Twenty of 'em, and
ammunition to correspond, under the whirligigs and the mud
dolls.'

'Heaven help you if you are caught with those things!' I
said. 'A Martini is worth her weight in silver among the
Pathans.'

27

'Fifteen hundred rupees of capital—every rupee we could beg, borrow, or steal—are invested on these two camels,' said Dravot. 'We won't get caught. We're going through the Khaiber with a regular caravan. Who'd touch a poor mad priest?'

'Have you got everything you want?' I asked, overcome with astonishment.

'Not yet, but we shall soon. Give us a memento of your kindness, *Brother*. You did me a service yesterday, and that time in Marwar. Half my Kingdom shall you have, as the saying is.' I slipped a small charm compass from my watch-chain and handed it up to the priest.

'Good-bye,' said Dravot, giving me hand cautiously. 'It's the last time we'll shake hands with an Englishman these many days. Shake hands with him, Carnehan,' he cried, as the second camel passed me.

Carnehan leaned down and shook hands. Then the camels passed away along the dusty road, and I was left alone to wonder. My eye could detect no failure in the disguises. The scene in Serai attested that they were complete to the native mind. There was just the chance, therefore, that Carnehan and Dravot would be able to wander through Afghanistan without detection. But, beyond, they would find death, certain and awful death.

Ten days later a native friend of mine, giving me the news of the day from Peshawur, wound up his letter with:—'There has been much laughter here on account of a certain mad priest who is going in his estimation to sell petty gauds and insignificant trinkets which he ascribes as great charms to H.H. the Amir of Bokhara. He passed through Peshawur and associated himself to the Second Summer caravan that goes to Kabul. The merchants are pleased because through superstition they imagine that such mad fellows bring good-fortune.'

The two, then, were beyond the Border. I would have prayed for them, but, that night, a real King died in Europe and demanded an obituary notice.

* * *

The wheel of the world swings through the same phases again

and again. Summer passed and winter thereafter, and came and passed again. The daily paper continued and I with it, and upon the third summer there fell a hot night, a night-issue, and a strained waiting for something to be telegraphed from the other side of the world, exactly as had happened before. A few great men had died in the past two years, the machines worked with more clatter, and some of the trees in the office garden were a few feet taller. But that was all the difference.

I passed over to the press-room, and went through just such a scene as I have already described. The nervous tension was stronger than it had been two years before, and I felt the heat more acutely. At three o'clock I cried, 'Print off,' and turned to go, when there crept to my chair what was left of a man. He was bent into a circle, his head was sunk between his shoulders, and he moved his feet one over the other like a bear. I could hardly see whether he walked or crawled—this rag-wrapped, whining cripple who addressed me by name, crying that he was come back, 'Can you give me a drink?' he whimpered. 'For the Lord's sake, give me a drink!'

I went back to the office, the man following with groans of pain, and I turned up the lamp.

'Don't you know me?' he gasped, dropping into a chair, and he turned his drawn face, surmounted by a shock of grey hair, to the light.

I looked at him intently. Once before had I seen eyebrows that met over the nose in an inch-broad black band, but for the life of me I could not tell where.

'I don't know you,' I said, handing him the whisky. 'What can I do for you?'

He took a gulp of the spirit raw, and shivered in spite of the suffocating heat.

'I've come back,' he repeated; 'and I was the King of Kafiristan—me and Dravot—crowned Kings we was! In this office we settled it—you setting there and giving us the books. I am Peachey—Peachey Taliaferro Carnehan, and you've been setting here ever since—O Lord!'

I was more than a little astonished, and expressed my feelings accordingly. 'It's true,' said Carnehan, with a dry cackle, nursing his feet, which were wrapped in rags. 'True as

29

gospel. Kings we were, with crowns upon our heads—me and Dravot—poor Dan—oh, poor, poor Dan, that would never take advice, not though I begged of him!'

'Take the whisky,' I said, 'and take your own time. Tell me all you can recollect of everything from beginning to end. You got across the border on your camels, Dravot dressed as a mad priest and you his servant. Do you remember that?'

'I ain't mad—yet, but I shall be that way soon. Of course I remember. Keep looking at me, or maybe my words will go all to pieces. Keep looking at me in my eyes and don't say anything.'

I leaned forward and looked into his face as steadily as I could. He dropped one hand upon the table and I grasped it by the wrist. It was twisted like a bird's claw, and upon the back was a ragged, red, diamond-shaped scar.

'No, don't look there. Look at *me*,' said Carnehan.

'That comes afterward, but for the Lord's sake don't distrack me. We left with that caravan, me and Dravot playing all sorts of antics to amuse the people we were with. Dravot used to make us laugh in the evenings when all the people were cooking their dinners—cooking their dinners, and . . . what did they do then? They lit little fires with sparks that went into Dravot's beard, and we all laughed—fit to die. Little red fires they was, going into Dravot's big red beard—so funny.' His eyes left mine and he smiled foolishly.

'You went as far as Jagdallak with that caravan,' I said, at a venture, 'after you had lit those fires. To Jagdallak, where you turned off to try to get into Kafiristan.'

'No, we didn't neither. What are you talking about? We turned off before Jagdallak, because we heard the roads was good. But they wasn't good enough for our two camels—mine and Dravot's. When we left the caravan, Dravot took off all his clothes and mine too, and said we would be heathen, because the Kafirs didn't allow Mohammedans to talk to them. So we dressed betwixt and between, and such a sight as Daniel Dravot I never saw yet nor expect to see again. He burned half his beard, and slung a sheep-skin over his shoulder, and shaved his head into patterns. He shaved mine, too, and made me wear outrageous things to look like a heathen. That was in a most mountaineous country, and our camels couldn't go along any more because of the mountains. They were tall and black, and coming home I saw them fight like wild goats— there are lots of goats in Kafiristan. And these mountains, they never keep still, no more than the goats. Always fighting they are, and don't let you sleep at night.'

'Take some more whisky,' I said, very slowly. 'What did you and Daniel Dravot do when the camels could go no further because of the rough roads that led into Kafiristan?'

'What did which do? There was a party called Peachey Taliaferro Carnehan that was with Dravot. Shall I tell you about him? He died out there in the cold. Slap from the bridge fell old Peachey, turning and twisting in the air like a penny whirligig that you can sell to the Amir.—No; they was two for three ha'pence, those whirligigs, or I am much mistaken and woful sore. And then these camels were no use, and Peachey said to Dravot—"For the Lord's sake, let's get out of this before our heads are chopped off," and with that they killed the camels all among the mountains, not having anything in particular to eat, but first they took off the boxes with the guns and the ammunition, till two men came along driving four mules. Dravot up and dances in front of them, singing,—"Sell me four mules." Says the first man,—"If you are rich enough to buy, you are rich enough to rob;" but before ever he could put his hand to his knife, Dravot breaks his neck over his knee, and the other party runs away. So Carnehan loaded the mules with the rifles that was taken off the camels, and together we starts forward into those bitter cold mountaineous parts, and never a road broader than the back of your hand.'

He paused for a moment, while I asked him if he could remember the nature of the country through which he had journeyed.

'I am telling you as straight as I can, but my head isn't as good as it might be. They drove nails through it to make me hear better how Dravot died. The country was mountaineous and the mules were most contrary, and the inhabitants was dispersed and solitary. They went up and up, and down and down, and that other party, Carnehan, was imploring of Dravot not to sing and whistle so loud, for fear of bringing down the tremenjus avalanches. But Dravot says that if a King couldn't sing it wasn't worth being King, and whacked the mules over the rump, and never took no heed for ten cold days. We came to a big level valley all among the mountains, and the mules were near dead, so we killed them, not having anything in special for them or us to eat. We sat upon the boxes, and played odd and even with the cartridges that was jolted out.

'Then ten men with bows and arrows ran down that valley, chasing twenty men with bows and arrows, and the row was tremenjus. They was fair men—fairer than you or me—with yellow hair and remarkable well built. Says Dravot, unpacking the guns—"This is the beginning of the business. We'll fight for the ten men," and with that he fires two rifles at the twenty men, and drops one of them at two hundred yards from the rock where we was sitting. The other men began to run but Carnehan and Dravot sits on the boxes picking them off at all ranges, up and down the valley. Then we goes up to the ten men that had run across the snow too, and they all falls down flat. Then he walks over them and kicks them, and then he lifts them up and shakes hands all round to make them friendly like. He calls them and gives them the boxes to carry, and waves his hand for all the world as though he was King already. They takes the boxes and him across the valley and up the hill into a pine wood on the top, where there was half a dozen big stone idols. Dravot he goes to the biggest—a fellow they call Imbra—and lays a rifle and a cartridge at his feet, rubbing his nose respectful with his own nose, patting him on the head, and saluting in front of it. He turns round to the men and nods his head, and says,—"That's all right. I'm in the know too, and all these old jim-jams are my friends." Then he opens his mouth and points down it, and when the first man brings him food, he says—"No," and when the second man brings him food, he says—"No;" but when one of the old priests and the boss of the village brings him food, he says— "Yes;" very haughty, and eats it slow. That was how we came to our first village, without any trouble, just as though we had tumbled from the skies. But we tumbled from one of those damned rope-bridges, you see, and you couldn't expect a man to laugh much after that.'

'Take some more whisky and go on,' I said. 'That was the first village you came into. How did you get to be King?'

'I wasn't King,' said Carnehan. 'Dravot he was the King, and a handsome man he looked with the gold crown on his head and all. Him and the other party stayed in that village, and every morning Dravot sat by the side of old Imbra, and the people came and worshipped. That was Dravot's order. Then a lot of men came into the valley, and Carnehan and Dravot picks them off with the rifles before they knew where they was, and runs down into the valley and up again the other side, and finds another village, same as the first one, and the people all falls down flat on their faces, and Dravot says,—"Now what is the trouble between you two villages?" and the people points to a woman, as fair as you or me, that was carried off, and Dravot takes her back to the first village and counts up the dead—eight there was. For each dead man Dravot pours a little milk on the ground and waves his arms like a whirligig and "That's all right," says he. Then he and Carnehan takes the big boss of each village by the arm and walks them down into the valley, and shows them how to scratch a line with a spear right down the valley, and gives each a sod of turf from both sides o' the line. Then all the people comes down and shouts like the devil and all, and Dravot says,—"Go and dig the land, and be fruitful and multiply," which they did, though they didn't understand. Then we asks the names of things in their lingo—bread and water and fire and idols and such, and Dravot leads the priest of each village up to the idol, and says he must sit there and judge the people, and if anything goes wrong he is to be shot.

'Next week they was all turning up the land in the valley as quiet as bees and much prettier, and the priests heard all the complaints and told Dravot in dumb show what it was about. "That's just the beginning," said Dravot. "They think we're Gods." He and Carnehan picks out twenty good men and shows them how to click off a rifle, and form fours, and a advance in line, and they was very pleased to do so, and clever to see the hang of it. Then he takes out his pipe and his baccy-pouch and leaves one at one village and one at the other, and off we two goes to see what was to be done in the next valley.

33

That was all rock, and there was a little village there, and Carnehan says,—"Send 'em to the old valley to plant," and takes 'em there and gives 'em some land that wasn't took before. They were a poor lot, and we blooded 'em with a kid before letting 'em into the new Kingdom. That was to impress the people, and then they settled down quiet, and Carnehan went back to Dravot who had got into another valley, all snow and ice and most mountaineous. There was no people there and the Army got afraid, so Dravot shoots one of them, and goes on till he finds some people in a village, and the Army explains that unless the people wants to be killed they had better not shoot their little matchlocks; for they had matchlocks. We make friends with the priest and I stays there alone with two of the Army, teaching the men how to drill, and a thundering big Chief comes across the snow with kettle-drums and horns twanging, because he heard there was a new God kicking about. Carnehan sights for the brown of the men half a mile across the snow and wings one of them. Then he sends a message to the Chief that, unless he wished to be killed, he must come and shake hands with me and leave his arms behind. The chief comes alone first, and Carnehan shakes hands with him and whirls his arms about, same as Dravot used, and very much surprised that Chief was, and strokes my eyebrows. Then Carnehan goes alone to the Chief, and asks him in dumb show if he had an enemy he hated. "I have," says the chief. So Carnehan weeds out the pick of his men, and sets the two of the Army to show them drill and at the end of two-weeks the men can manoeuvre about as well as Volunteers. So he marches with the Chief to a great big plain on the top of a mountain, and the Chief's men rushes into a village and takes it; we three Martinis firing into the brown of the enemy. So we took that village too, and I gives the Chief a rag from my coat and says, "Occupy till I come:" which was scriptural. By way of a reminder, when me and the Army was eighteen hundred yards away, I drops a bullet near him standing on the snow, and all the people falls flat on their faces. Then I sends a letter to Dravot, wherever he be by land or by sea.'

At the risk of throwing the creature out of train I interrupted,—'How could you write a letter up yonder?'

'The letter?—Oh!—The letter! Keep looking at me between the eyes, please. It was a string-talk letter, that we'd learned the way of it from a blind beggar in the Punjab.'

I remember that there had once come to the office a blind man with a knotted twig and a piece of string which he wound round the twig according to some cypher of his own. He could, after the lapse of days or hours, repeat the sentence which he had reeled up. He had reduced the alphabet to eleven primitive sounds; and tried to teach me his method, but failed.

'I sent that letter to Dravot,' said Carnehan; 'and told him to come back because this Kingdom was growing too big for me to handle, and then I struck for the first valley, to see how the priests were working. They called the village we took along with the Chief, Bashkai, and the first village we took, Er-Heb. The priests at Er-Heb was doing all right, but they had a lot of pending cases about land to show me, and some men from another village had been firing arrows at night. I went out and looked for that village and fired four rounds at it from a thousand yards. That used all the cartridges I cared to spend, and I waited for Dravot, who had been away two or three months, and I kept my people quiet.

'One morning I heard the devil's own noise of drums and horns, and Dan Dravot marches down the hill with his Army and a tail of hundreds of men, and, which was the most amazing—a great gold crown on his head. "My Gord, Carnehan," says Daniel, "This is a tremendous business, and we've got the whole country as far as it's worth having. I am the son of Alexander by Queen Semiramis, and you're my younger brother and a God too! It's the biggest thing we've ever seen. I've been marching and fighting for six weeks with the Army, and every footy little village for fifty miles has come in rejoiceful; and more than that, I've got the key of the whole show, as you'll see, and I've got a crown for you! I told 'em to make two of 'em at a place called Shu, where the gold lies in the rock like suet in mutton. Gold I've seen, and turquoise I've kicked out of the cliffs, and there's garnets in the sands of the river, and here's a chunk of amber that a man brought me. Call up all the priests and, here, take your crown."

'One of the men opens a black hair bag and I slips the

crown on. It was too small and too heavy, but I wore it for the glory. Hammered gold it was—five pound weight, like a hoop of a barrel.

"'Peachey,' says Dravot, 'we don't want to fight no more. The Craft's the trick so help me!' and he brings forward that same Chief that I left at Bashkai—Billy Fish we called him afterward, because he was so like Billy Fish that drove the big tank-engine at Mach on the Bolan in the old days. 'Shake hands with him,' says Dravot, and I shook hands and nearly dropped, for Billy Fish gave me the Grip. I said nothing, but tried him with the Fellow Craft Grip. He answers, all right, and I tried the Master's Grip, but that was a slip. 'A Fellow Craft he is!' I says to Dan. 'Does he know the word?' 'He does,' says Dan, 'and all the priests know. It's a miracle! The Chiefs and the priests can work a Fellow Craft Lodge in a way that's very like ours, and they've cut the marks on the rocks, but they don't know the Third Degree, and they've come to find out. It's Gord's Truth. I've known these long years that the Afghans knew up to the Fellow Craft Degree, but this is a miracle. A God and a Grand-Master of the Craft am I, and a Lodge in the Third Degree I will open, and we'll raise the head priests and the Chiefs of the villages.'

"'It's against all the law,' I says, 'holding a Lodge without warrant from any one; and we never held office in any Lodge.'

"'It's a master-stroke of policy,' says Dravot. 'It means running the country as easy as a four-wheeled bogy on a down grade. We can't stop to inquire now, or they'll turn against us. I've forty Chiefs at my heel, and passed and raised according to their merit they shall be. Billet these men on the villages and see that we run up a Lodge of some kind. The temple of Imbra will do for the Lodge-room. The women must make aprons as you show them. I'll hold a levee of Chiefs tonight and Lodge to-morrow.'

'I was fair run off my legs, but I wasn't such a fool as not to see what a pull this Craft business gave us. I showed the priests' families how to make aprons of the degrees, but for Dravot's apron the blue border and marks was made of turquoise lumps on white hide, not cloth. We took a great square stone in the temple for the Master's chair, and little

stones for the officers' chairs, and painted the black pavement
with white squares, and did what we could to make things
regular.

'At the levee which was held that night on the hillside with
big bonfires, Dravot gives out that him and me were Gods and
sons of Alexander, and Past Grand-Masters in the Craft, and
was come to make Kafiristan a country wherein every man
should eat in peace and drink in quiet, and specially obey us.
Then the Chiefs come round to shake hands, and they was so
hairy and white and fair it was just shaking hands with old
friends. We gave them names according as they was like men
we had known in India—Billy Fish, Holly Dilworth, Pikky
Kergan that was Bazaar-master when I was at Mhow, and so
on and so on.

'The *most* amazing miracle was at Lodge next night. One of
the old priests was watching us continuous, and I felt uneasy,
for I know we'd have to fudge the Ritual, and I didn't know
what the men knew. The old priest was a stranger come in
from beyond the village of Bashkai. The minute Dravot puts on
the Master's apron that the girls had made for him, the priest
fetches a whoop and a howl, and tries to overturn the stone
that Dravot was sitting on. "It's all up now," I says. "That
comes of meddling with the Craft without warrant!" Dravot
never winked an eye, not when ten priests took and tilted over
the Grand-Master's chair—which was to say the stone of Imbra.
The priest begins rubbing the bottom end of it to clear away
the black dirt, and presently he shows all the other priests the
Master's Mark, same as was on Dravot's apron, cut into the
stone. Not even the priests of the temple of Imbra knew it was
there. The old chap falls flat on his face at Dravot's feet and
kisses 'em. "Luck again," says Dravot, across the Lodge to me,
"they say it's the missing Mark that no one could understand
the why of. We're more than safe now." Then he bangs the butt
of his gun for a gavel and says:—"By virtue of the authority
vested in me by my own right hand and the help of Peachey,
I declare myself Grand-Master of all Freemasonry in Kafiristan
in this the Mother Lodge o' the country, and King of Kafiristan
equally with Peachey!" At that he puts on his crown and I puts
on mine—I was doing Senior Warden—and we opens the

Lodge in most ample form. It was an amazing miracle! The priests moved in Lodge through the first two degrees almost without telling, as if the memory was coming back to them. After that, Peachey and Dravot raised such as was worthy— high priests and Chiefs of far-off villages. Billy Fish was the first and I can tell you we scared the soul out of him. It was not in any way according to Rituals, but it served our turn. We didn't raise more than ten of the biggest men because we didn't want to make the Degree common. And they was clamouring to be raised.

'"In another six months," says Dravot, "we'll hold another Communication and see how you are working." Then he asks them about their villages, and learns that they was fighting one against the other and were fair sick and tired of it. And when they wasn't doping that they was fighting with the Mohammedans. "You can fight those when they come into our country," says Dravot. "Tell off every tenth man of your tribes for a Frontier guard, and send two hundred at a time to this valley to be drilled. Nobody is going to be shot or speared any more so long as he does well, and I know that you won't cheat me because you're white people—sons of Alexander—and not like common, black Mohammedans. You are *my* people and by God," says he, running off into English at the end—"I'll make a damned fine Nation of you, or I'll die in the making!"

'I can't tell all we did for the next six months because Dravot did a lot I couldn't see the hang of, and he learned their lingo in a way I never could. My work was to help the people plough, and now and again go out with some of the Army and see what the other villages were doing, and make 'em throw rope-bridges across the ravines which cut up the country horrid. Dravot was very kind to me, but when he walked up and down in the pine wood pulling that bloody red beard of his with both fists I knew he was thinking plans I could not advise him about, and I just waited for orders.

'But Dravot never showed me disrespect before the people. They were afraid of me and the Army, but they loved Dan. He was the best of friends with the priests and the Chiefs; but any one could come across the hills with a complaint and Dravot would hear him out fair, and call four priests together and say what was to be done. He used to call in Billy Fish from Bashkai, and Pikky Kergan from Shu, and an old Chief we called Kafuzelum—it was like enough to his real name—and hold councils with 'em when there was any fighting to be done in small villages. That was his Council of War, and the four priests of Bashkai, Shu, Khawak, and Madora was his Privy Council. Between the lot of 'em they send me, with forty men and twenty rifles, and sixty men carrying turquoises, into the Ghorband country to buy those hand-made Martini rifles, that come out of the Amir's workshops at Kabul, from one of the Amir's Herati regiments that would have sold the very teeth out of their mouths for turquoises.

'I stayed in Ghorband a month, and gave the Governor there the pick of my baskets for hush-money, and bribed the Colonel of the regiment some more, and, between the two and the tribes-people, we got more than a hundred hand-made Martinis, a hundred good Kohat Jezails, that'll throw to six hundred yards, and forty man-loads of very bad ammunition for the rifles. I came back with what I had, and distributed 'em among the men that the Chiefs sent to me to drill. Dravot was too busy to attend to those things, but the old Army that we first made helped me, and we turned out five hundred men that could drill, and two hundred that knew how to hold arms pretty straight. Even those cork-screwed, hand-made guns was a miracle to them. Dravot talked big about powder-shops and factories, walking up and down in the pine wood when the winter was coming on.

'"I won't make a Nation," says he, "I'll make an Empire! These men aren't niggers; they're English! Look at their eyes— look at their mouths. Look at the way they stand up. They sit on chairs in their own houses. They're the Lost Tribes, or something like it, and they've grown to be English. I'll take a census in the spring if the priests don't get frightened. There must be a fair two million of 'em in these hills. The villages are full o' little children. Two million people—two hundred and fifty thousand fighting men—and all English! They only want the rifles and a little drilling. Two hundred and fifty thousand men, ready to cut in on Russia's right flank when she tries for India! Peachey, man," he says, chewing his beard in great hunks, "we shall be Emperors—Emperors of the Earth! Rajah Brooke will be a suckling to us. I'll treat with the Viceroy on equal terms. I'll ask him to send me twelve picked English— twelve that I know of—to help us govern a bit. There's Mackray, Sergeant-pensioner at Segowli—many's the good dinner he's given me, and his wife a pair of trousers. There's Donkin, the Warder of Tounghoo Jail; there's hundreds that I could lay my hand on if I was in India. The Viceroy shall do it for me. I'll send a man through in the spring for those men, and I'll write for a dispensation from the Grand Lodge for what I've done as Grand-Master. That—and all the Sniders that'll be thrown out when the native troops in India take up the Martini. They'll be worn smooth, but they'll do for fighting in these hills. Twelve English, a hundred thousand Sniders run through the Amir's country in driblets—I'd be content with twenty thousand in one year—and we'd be an Empire. When everything was shipshape, I'd hand over the crown—this crown I'm wearing now—to Queen Victoria on my knees, and she'd say: Rise up, Sir Daniel Dravot. Oh, it's big! It's big, I tell you! But there's so much to be done in every place—Bashkai, Khawak, Shu, and everywhere else."

"'What is it?' I says. "There are no more men coming in to be drilled this autumn. Look at those fat, black clouds. They're bringing the snow."

"'It isn't that," says Daniel, putting his hand very hard on my shoulder; "and I don't wish to say anything that's against you, for no other living man would have followed me and made me what I am as you have done. You're a first-class Commander-in-Chief, and the people know you; but—it's a big country, and somehow you can't help me, Peachey, in the way I want to be helped."

"'Go to your blasted priests, then!" I said, and I was sorry when I made that remark, but it did hurt me sore to find Daniel talking so superior when I'd drilled all the men, and done all he told me.

"'Don't let's quarrel, Peachey," says Daniel, without cursing. "You're a King too, and the half of this Kingdom is yours; but can't you see, Peachey, we want cleverer men than us now— three or four of 'em, that we can scatter about for our Deputies.

It's a hugeous great State, and I can't always tell the right thing to do, and I haven't time for all I want to do, and here's the winter coming on and all." He put half his beard into his mouth, and it was as red as the gold of his crown.

"'I'm sorry, Daniel," says I. "I've done all I could. I've drilled the men and shown the people how to stack their oats better; and I've brought in those tinware rifles from Ghorband—but I know what you're driving at. I take it Kings always feel oppressed that way."

"'There's another thing too," says Dravot, walking up and down. "The winter's coming and these people won't be giving much trouble, and if they do we can't move about. I want a wife."

"'For Gord's sake leave the women alone!" I says. "We've both got all the work we can, though I *am* a fool. Remember the Contrack, and keep clear o' women."

"'The Contrack only lasted till such time as we was Kings; and Kings we have been these months past," says Dravot, weighing his crown in his hand. "You go get a wife too, Peachey—a nice, strappin', plump girl that'll keep you warm in the winter. They're prettier than English girls, and we can take the pick of 'em. Boil 'em once or twice in hot water, and they'll come as fair as chicken and ham."

"'Don't tempt me!" I says. "I will not have any dealings with a woman not till we are a dam' side more settled than we are now. I've been doing the work o' two men, and you've been doing the work o' three. Let's lie off a bit, and see if we can get some better tobacco from Afghan country and run in some good liquor; but no women."

"'Who's talking o' *women*?" says Dravot. "I said *wife*—a Queen to breed a King's son for the King. A Queen out of the strongest tribe, that'll make them your blood-brothers, and that'll lie by your side and tell you all the people thinks about you and their own affairs. That's what I want."

"'Do you remember that Bengali woman I kept at Mogul Serai when I was a plate-layer?" says I. "A fat lot o' good she was to me. She taught me the lingo and one or two other things; but what happened? She ran away with the Station Master's servant and half my month's pay. Then she turned up at Dadur Junction in tow of a half-caste, and had the impidence to say I was her husband—all among the drivers in the running-shed!"

"'We've done with that," says Dravot. "These women are whiter than you or me, and a Queen I will have for the winter months."

"'For the last time o' asking, Dan, do *not*," I says. "It'll only bring us harm. The Bible says that Kings ain't to waste their strength on women,' specially when they've got a new raw Kingdom to work over."

"'For the last time of answering I will," said Dravot, and he went away through the pine-trees looking like a big red devil. The low sun hit his crown and beard on one side and the two blazed like hot coals.

'But getting a wife was not as easy as Dan thought. He put it before the Council, and there was no answer till Billy Fish said that he'd better ask the girls. Dravot damned them all round. "What's wrong with me?" he shouts, standing by the idol Imbra. "Am I a dog or am I not enough of a man for your wenches? Haven't I put the shadow of my hand over this country? Who stopped the last Afghan raid?" It was me really, but Dravot was too angry to remember. "Who brought your guns? Who repaired the bridges? Who's the Grand-Master of the sign cut in the stone?" and he thumped his hand on the block that he used to sit on in Lodge, and at Council, which opened like Lodge always. Billy Fish said nothing and no more did the others. "Keep your hair on, Dan," said I; "and ask the girls. That's how it's done at Home, and these people are quite English."

"'The marriage of the King is a matter of State," says Dan, in a white-hot rage, for he could feel, I hope, that he was going against his better mind. He walked out of the Council-room, and the others sat still, looking at the ground.

"'Billy Fish," says I to the Chief of Bashkai, "what's the difficulty here? A straight answer to a true friend." "You know," says Billy Fish. "How should a man tell you who knows everything? How can daughters of men marry Gods or Devils? It's not proper."

'I remember something like that in the Bible; but, if, after seeing us as long as they had they still believed we were Gods, it wasn't for me to undeceive them.

'"A God can do anything," says I. "If the King is fond of a girl he'll not let her die." "She'll have to," said Billy Fish. "There are all sorts of Gods and Devils in these mountains, and now and again a girl marries one of them and isn't seen any more. Besides, you two know the Mark cut in the stone. Only the Gods know that. We thought you were men till you showed the sign of the Master."

'I wished then that we had explained about the loss of the genuine secrets of a Master-Mason at the first go-off; but I said nothing. All that night there was a blowing of horns in a little dark temple half-way down the hill, and I heard a girl crying fit to die. One of the priests told us that she was being prepared to marry the King.

'"I'll have no nonsense of that kind," says Dan. "I don't want to interfere with your customs, but I'll take my own wife." "The girl's a little bit afraid," says the priest. "She thinks she's going to die, and they are a-heartening of her up down in the temple."

'"Hearten her very tender, then," says Dravot, "or I'll hearten you with the butt of a gun so that you'll never want to be heartened again." He licked his lips, did Dan, and stayed up walking about more than half the night, thinking of the wife that he was going to get in the morning. I wasn't any means comfortable, for I knew that dealings with a woman in foreign parts, though you was a crowned King twenty times over, could not but be risky. I got up very early in the morning while Dravot was asleep, and I saw the priests talking together in whispers, and the Chiefs talking together too, and they looked at me out of the corners of their eyes.

'"What is up, Fish?" I says to the Bashkai man, who was wrapped up in his furs and looking splendid to behold.

'"I can't rightly say," says he; "but if you can induce the King to drop all this nonsense about marriage, you'll be doing him and me and yourself a great service."

'"That I do believe," says I. "But sure, you know, Billy, as well as me, having fought against and for us, that the King and me are nothing more than two of the finest men that

God Almighty ever made. Nothing more, I do assure you."

"'That may be," says Billy fish, "and yet I should be sorry if it was." He sinks his head upon his great fur cloak for a minute and thinks. "King," says he, 'be you man or God or Devil, I'll stick by you to-day. I have twenty of my men with me, and they will follow me. We'll go to Bashkai until the storm blows over."

'A little snow had fallen in the night, and everything was white except the greasy far clouds that blew down and down from the north. Dravot came out with his crown on his head, swinging his arms and stamping his feet, and looking more pleased than Punch.

"'For the last time, drop it, Dan," says I, in a whisper. "Billy Fish here says that there will be a row."

"'A row among my people!" says Dravot. "Not much. Peachey, you're a fool not to get a wife too. Where's the girl?" says he, with a voice as loud as the braying of a jackass. "Call up all the Chiefs and priests, and let the Emperor see if his wife suits him."

'There was no need to call any one. They were all there leaning on their guns and spears round the clearing in the centre of the pine wood. A deputation of priests went down to the little temple to bring up the girl, and the horns blew up fit to wake the dead. Billy Fish saunters round and gets as close to Daniel as he could, and behind him stood his twenty men with matchlocks. Not a man of them under six feet. I was next to Dravot, and behind me as twenty men of the regular Army. Up comes the girl, and a strapping wench she was, covered with silver and turquoises but white as death, and looking back every minute at the priests.

"'She'll do," said Dan, looking her over. "What's to be afraid of, lass? Come and kiss me." He puts his arm round her. She shuts her eyes, gives a bit of squeak, and down goes her face in the side of Dan's flaming red beard.

"'The slut's bitten me!" says he, clapping his hand to his neck, and, sure enough, his hand was red with blood. Billy Fish and two of his matchlock-men catches hold of Dan by the shoulders and drags him into the Bashkai lot while the priests howls in their lingo,—"Neither God nor Devil but a man!" I was all taken aback, for a priest cut at me in front, and the Army behind began firing into the Bashkai men.

"'God A-might!' says Dan. "What is the meaning o' this?"

"'Come back! Come away!' says Billy Fish. "Ruin and Mutiny is the matter. We'll break for Bashkai if we can."

'I tried to give some sort of orders to my men—the men o' the regular Army—but it was no use, so I fired into the brown of 'em with an English Martini and drilled three beggars in a line. The valley was full of shouting, howling creatures, and every soul was shrieking, "Not a God nor a Devil but only a man!" The Bashkai troops stuck to Billy Fish all they were worth, but their matchlocks wasn't half as good as the Kabul breech-loaders, and four of them dropped. Dan was bellowing like a bull, for he was very wrathy; and Billy Fish had a hard job to prevent him running out at the crowd.

"'We can't stand," says Billy Fish. "Make a run for it down the valley! The whole place is against us." The matchlock-men ran, and we went down the valley in spite of Dravot's protestations. He was swearing horribly and crying out that he was a King. The priests rolled great stones on us, and the regular Army fired hard, and there wasn't more than six men, not counting Dan, Billy Fish, and Me, that came down to the bottom of the Valley alive.

'Then they stopped firing and the horns in the temple blew again. "Come away—for Gord's sake come away!" says Billy Fish. "They'll send runners out to all the villages before ever we get to Bashkai. I can protect you there, but I can't do anything now."

'My own notion is that Dan began to go mad in his head from that hour. He stared up and down like a stuck pig. Then he was all for walking back alone and killing the priests with his bare hands; which he could have done. "An Emperor am I," says Daniel, "and next year I shall be a Knight of the Queen."

"'All right, Dan," says I; "but come along now while there's time."

"'It's your fault," says he, "for not looking after your Army better. There was mutiny in the midst, and you didn't know— you damned engine-driving, plate-laying, missionary's-pass-hunting hound!" He sat upon a rock and called me every foul name he could lay tongue to. I was too heart-sick to care, though it was all his foolishness that brought the smash.

"'I'm sorry, Dan," says I, "but there's no accounting for natives. This business is our Fifty-Seven. Maybe we'll make something out of it yet, when we've got to Bashkai."

"'Let's get to Bashkai, then," says Dan, 'and, by God, when I come back here again I'll sweep the valley so there isn't a bug in a blanket left!"

'We walked all that day, and all that night Dan was stumping up and down on the snow, chewing his beard and muttering to himself.

"'There's no hope o' getting clear," said Billy Fish. "The priests will have sent runners to the villages to say that you are only men. Why didn't you stick on as Gods till things was more settled? I'm a dead man," says Billy Fish, and he throws himself down on the snow and begins to pray to his Gods.

'Next morning we was in a cruel bad country—all up and down, no level ground at all, and no food either. The six Bashkai men looked at Billy Fish hungry-wise as if they wanted to ask something, but they said never a word. At noon we came to the top of a flat mountain all covered with snow, and when we climbed up into it, behold, there was an Army in position waiting in the middle!

"'The runners have been very quick," says Billy Fish, with a little bit of a laugh. "They are waiting for us."

'Three or four men began to fire from the enemy's side, and a chance shot took Daniel in the calf of the leg. That brought him to his senses. He looks across the snow at the Army, and sees the rifles that we had brought into the country.

"'We're done for," says he. "They are Englishmen, these people,—and it's my blasted nonsense that has brought you to this. Get back, Billy Fish, and take your men away; you've done what you could, and now cut for it. Carnehan," says he, "shake hands with me and go along with Billy. Maybe they won't kill you. I'll go and meet 'em alone. It's me that did it. Me, the King!"

"'Go!" says I. "Go to Hell, Dan. I'm with you here. Billy Fish, you clear out, and we two will meet those folk."

"'I'm a Chief," says Billy Fish, quite quiet. "I stay with you. My men can go."

'The Bashkai fellows didn't wait for a second word but ran off, and Dan and Me and Billy Fish walked across to where the drums were drumming and the horns were horning. It was cold—awful cold. I've got that cold in the back of my head now. There's a lump of it there.'

The punkah-coolies had gone to sleep. Two kerosene lamps were blazing in the office, and the perspiration poured down my face and splashed on the blotter as I leaned forward. Carnehan was shivering, and I feared that his mind might go. I wiped my face, took a fresh grip of the piteously mangled hands, and said:—'What happened after that?'

The momentary shift of my eyes had broken the clear current.

'What was you pleased to say?' whined Carnehan. 'They took them without any sound. Not a little whisper all along the snow, not though the King knocked down the first man that set hand on him—not though old Peachey fired his last cartridge into the brown of 'em. Not a single solitary sound did those swines make. They just closed up tight, and I tell you their furs stunk. There was a man called Billy Fish, a good friend of us all, and they cut his throat, Sir, then and there, like a pig; and the King kicks up the bloody snow and says:—"We've had a dashed fine run for our money. What's coming next?" But Peachey, Peachey Taliaferro, I tell you, Sir, in confidence as betwixt two friends, he lost his head, Sir. No, he didn't neither. The King lost his head, so he did, all along o' one of those cunning rope-bridges. Kindly let me have the paper-cutter, Sir. It tilted this way. They marched him a mile across that snow to a rope-bridge over a ravine with a river at the bottom. You may have seen such. They prodded him behind like an ox. "Damn your eyes!" says thy King. "D'you suppose I can't die like a gentleman?" He turns to Peachey—Peachey that was crying like a child. "I've brought you to this, Peachey," says he. "Brought you out of your happy life to be killed in Kafiristan, where you was late Commander-in-Chief of the Emperor's forces. Say you forgive me, Peachey." "I do," says Peachey. "Fully and freely do I forgive you, Dan." "Shake hands, Peachey," says he. "I'm going now." Out he goes, looking neither right nor left, and when he was plumb in the middle of

47

those dizzy dancing ropes. "Cut, you beggars," he shouts; and they cut, and old Dan fell, turning round and round and round twenty thousand miles, for he took half an hour to fall till he struck the water, and I could see his body caught on a rock with the gold crown close beside.

'But do you know what they did to Peachey between two pine trees? They crucified him, Sir, as Peachey's hand will show. They used wooden pegs for his hands and his feet; and he didn't die. He hung there and screamed, and they took him down next day, and said it was a miracle that he wasn't dead. They took him down—poor old Peachey that hadn't done them any harm—that hadn't done them any . . . . '

He rocked to and fro and wept bitterly, wiping his eyes with the back of his scarred hands and moaning like a child for some ten minutes.

'They was cruel enough to feed him up in the temple, because they said he was more of a God than old Daniel that was a man. Then they turned him out on the snow, and told him to go home, and Peachey came home in about a year, begging along the roads quite safe; for Daniel Dravot he walked before and said:—"Come along, Peachey. It's a big thing we're doing." The mountains they danced at night, and the mountains they tried to fall on Peachey's head, but Dan he held up his hand, and Peachey came along bent double. He never let go of Dan's hand, and he never let go of Dan's head. They gave it to him as a present in the temple to remind him not to come again, and though the crown was pure gold and Peachey was starving, never would Peachey sell the same. You knew Dravot, Sir! You knew Right Worshipful Brother Dravot! Look at him now!'

He fumbled in the mass of rags round his bent waist; brought out a black horsehair bag embroidered with silver thread; and shook therefrom on to my table—the dried, withered head of Daniel Dravot! The morning sun that had long been paling the lamps struck the red beard and blind sunken eyes; struck, too, a heavy circlet of gold studded with raw turquoises, that Carnehan placed tenderly on the battered temples.

'You behold now,' said Carnehan, 'the Emperor in his habit as he lived—the King of Kafiristan with his crown upon his head. Poor old Daniel that was a monarch once!'

I shuddered, for in spite of defacements manifold, I recognized the head of the man of Marwar Junction. Carnehan rose to go. I attempted to stop him. He was not fit to walk abroad. 'Let me take away the whisky and give me a little money,' he gasped. 'I was a King once. I'll go to the Deputy Commissioner and ask to set in the Poorhouse till I get my health. No, thank you, I can't wait till you get a carriage for me. I've urgent private affairs—in the south—at Marwar'

He shambled out of the office and departed in the direction of the Deputy Commissioner's house. That day at noon I had occasion to go down the blinding hot Mall, and I saw a crooked man crawling along the white dust of the roadside, his hat in his hand, quavering dolorously after the fashion of street-singers at Home. There was not a soul in sight and he was out of all possible earshot of the houses. And he sang through his nose, turning his head from right to left:

> The Son of Man goes forth to war,
> A golden crown to gain;
> His blood-red banner streams afar—
> Who follows in his train?

I waited to hear no more, but put the poor wretch into my carriage and drove him off to the nearest missionary for eventual transfer to the Asylum. He repeated the hymn twice while he was with me whom he did not in the least recognize, and I left him singing it to the missionary.

Two days later I inquired after his welfare of the Superintendent of the Asylum.

'He was admitted suffering from sun-stroke. He died early yesterday morning,' said the Superintendent. 'Is it true that he was half an hour bareheaded in the sun at midday?'

'Yes,' said I, 'but do you happen to know if he had anything upon him by any chance when he died?'

'Not to my knowledge,' said the Superintendent.

And there the matter rests.

By Cow-Catcher and Trolley

Anonymous

THERE ARE MORE WAYS THAN ONE
of travelling on a railway, but they do not come the way of all.
It must have been a desire of every boy and indeed of many a
man to ride in the cab of an engine not to speak of a journey
upon the cow-catcher, while, for some, even the slow hand-
pushed trolley has a certain fascination. And in this world,
when anticipation is so often the better part of a thing, it is a
consolation to find that these boyish ideals of the joyrides to be
obtained on engines and trolleys are not entirely incapable of
fulfilment.

When you clamber to the foot-plate and survey the world
from a proud height not only physically but mentally—for you
tell yourself that it is only privileged persons who can enjoy the
experience you are about to undergo—the feeling is somewhat
akin to that of mounting a seventeen-hands horse—at least that
is what suggests itself. One is so high up in the world that
things seem dwarfed, but the size of the locomotive itself—an
elephantine monster from the ground—decreases perceptibly.
The next impression is the change of the field of vision. One is
used to a side view from a train; up here in the cab one gets
a sight of the line from a new angle and along the great black
shiny flank of the 'iron horse.' One is surprised somewhat at
both the extent and smallness of the country taken in; the long
stretch of open line with the converging rails waiting to be

pinched off into nothingness where the perspective takes final effect and the extraordinary reduction round curves in cuttings or jungle. What with the smokestack and the shoulder of the engine the view from the outer side of the curve is as limited as that on the inner. And one no longer wonders why, at times, there is so much whistling from the engine. The driver is but giving a warning to trolleymen and permanent-way repairers of his presence, for it is astonishing how quietly a train may steal up when a cutting softens the sound of the reverberating snorts of the locomotive and deadens the roar of the wheels. On a downgrade, with steam shut off, a heavy train will slip along with comparatively no sound whatever to those on the line ahead. Hence the warning note when a sharp curve is at hand.

But perhaps the most startling revelation is the strenuous life of the stoker. He adds fuel to the roaring leaping yellow flames with their background of glowing red embers on the average once very two minutes. Open swings the door of the fire box and a great heat scorches the body and limbs of those on the foot-plate. A ruddy light gleams in the dark corners of the cab. The heat seems to glance and flicker about one as the flames dance within their bright prison. But the fireman, regardless of the tremendous heat, of the glare that seems to sear the eye-balls, of the scorching wind that dries up the throat, is flinging in shovelfuls of coal, sprinkling them to right and left, distributing them evenly over the surface of the fire. His last shovelful is bestowed with a neat turn of the wrist as the shovel rests on the edge of the furnace-opening that flings a last layer in all directions. Clang! The heat and the glare are cut off as if by a magic, and the fireman goes to the side of the cab for a breath of fresh air; but in sixty seconds he is back again. Clang! Again that spectacle of ravening flames awaiting food, that terrible scorching, that ghastly glare; again the speedy spadework; again the grateful relief. So the fireman gets through his spell, and if ever a man earned his pay it is surely he. Behind him a khalassi is shovelling coal down from the tender, breaking up the food for the giant's searing maw; sweeping up and keeping everything ship-shape. The driver, his eyes on the line, his hand within easy reach of the whistle cord, is a busy man, but his business is more that of the brain and the eye than of the hand. The general impression of life on the foot-plate is that it is one of the most strenuous modern conditions have yet produced.

But travelling in the cab must give place so far as new sensations go to riding on the cow-catcher. Here you are as a pioneer; the first explorer in a new country; the advance guard of many things. Seated on the steel platform beside the couplings you have the warmth of the engine at your back, but the wind of your passage chills you through. The actual riding is comfortable enough barring a crampy feeling where your knees touch the edges of steel and a desire to stretch your legs and lean back that needs to be kept in hand. But you forget these little disabilities in the joy of a new movement; in the whistle of the air about your ears; in the thunder of the ordered power behind. Far ahead of you stretches the steel road, two shining bars that gleam and glitter. And as fast as your speed eats them up new distances are unrolling, just as a great carpet might be flung out by the skilful hand of a giant shopman. The scenery flits by like a cinematograph picture; new vistas open out in front; the sleepers rise up to strike you, but they are always too late. Here the train is clearing miles of ghats and the atmosphere is undergoing curious changes of temperature. Deep in the cuttings the air is damp and cool—almost shrewd; out in the open the normal heat returns, tempered by the flow of air. Round the curves the whistle shrieks in your ear; on the down grade you can enjoy the smooth travelling as the great load of steel and wood and human life slips along under its own momentum; climbing, the engine pulsates, throbs, bounds under the impulse of the drive and clatter of the piston rods. Darkness is drawing in and the signal lights begin to glimmer amid the gloom of the forest. The air grows colder and in the jungles it nips you through until you long for warmer clothing and warmer air. The night mists are creeping up; shadows are falling across the line; a cheeky jackal refuses to move, despite the deep-throated blast of the whistle, until the train is thirty yards from him and then he bounds up the cutting; the sky darkens and the glow of the sunset deepens. The rush of the air is driving tears from your eyes and demands the application of your handkerchief; the great locomotive is thrusting itself along with a thunderous roar and over the great black shoulder of the engine the evening star gleams in a dying field of saffron.

After a journey in a cow-catcher a trolley-ride would seem slow by comparison. But there are such things as motor-trollies and a motor-trolley is a distinct sensation. It is a motor chassis on four small railway wheels but with no steering gear. But what it lacks in appearance it makes up in speed, vibration, and clatter, and the man who said that when you had finished you would not be able to hear anyone speak was not exaggerating. The most curious thing about a motor-trolley is that your feet are nearly touching the track, and the result is that sleepers and ballast seem to be preparing for a combined attack upon your legs which they are always too late to deliver. Every sleeper, every stone, raises itself to strike, but slips away, indistinguishable in the mist of speed. Over bridges, the gaunt black sleepers jump up singly one after the other, only to be merged into a mass as they surge beneath you. Conversation is impossible. A shouted remark, directed by a curved hand to your ear, comes faintly as a lengthy hail; your own voice in replay sounds like a wheezy time-expired gramophone doing its utmost with a worn-out needle on a cracked, uneven record. And all the time the hot air is dashing by at thirty miles an hour, you are swaying from side to side as the trolley responds to her driving power and the rattle of the wheels on the rails and the rattle of the engine combine in one hoarse roar.

After this a push trolley is a simple affair. And yet it has its points. For one thing conversation is possible. One might debate the Baconian theory, or discourse on philosophy without distraction while the trolley slips along the line. And yet the trolley is wonderful—or at least its coolies are. To most of us walking on the metals would be a feat of balancing that would entitle us to appear as a turn on the 'halls.' We should achieve it only by much swaying and beating of the air with the hands. But the trolley-men in India not only progress along the lines, but they run; one foot over the other, and they never put a foot wrong. Moreover, they cut along at an amazing rate, running with the body well forward and the long stride that tells of the

athlete. And when they have the trolley going well they swing
up to the platform and sit on the handle-bar with which they
have been pushing; only to drop unerringly back again, feet in
the correct position on the line, when the speed shows signs of
slackening.

The Bold 'Prentice

Rudyard Kipling

THIS STORY IS VERY MUCH OF THE
same sort as 'An Unqualified Pilot,' and shows that, when any one
is really keen on his job, he will generally find some older man who
is even keener than he, who will give him help and instruction that
could not be found in a whole library of books. Olaf Swanson's book
of 'Road Locos Repair or the Young Driver's Vademecome,' was well
known in the Railway sheds in its day, and was written in the
queerest English ever printed. But it told useful facts and, as you will
see, saved a train at a pinch. It may be worth noticing that young
Ottley's chance did not come to him till he had worked on and among
engine-repairs for some five or six years and was well-grounded in
practical knowledge of his subject.

* * *

Young Ottley's father came to Calcutta in 1857 as fireman on
the first locomotive ever run by the D.I.R., which was then the
largest Indian railway. All his life he spoke broad Yorkshire,
but young Ottley, being born in India, naturally talked the
clipped sing-song that is used by the half-castes and English-
speaking natives. When he was fifteen years old the D.I.R. took
him into their service as an apprentice in the Locomotive Repair
Department of the Ajaibpore workshops, and he became one of
a gang of three or four white men and nine or ten natives.

There were scores of such gangs, each with its hoisting and overhead cranes, jack-screws, vises and lathes, as separate as separate shops, and their work was to mend locomotives and make the apprentices behave. But the apprentices threw nuts at one another, chalked caricatures of unpopular foremen on buffer-bars and discarded boilers, and did as little work as they possibly could.

They were nearly all sons of old employees, living with their parents in the white bungalows of Steam Road or Church Road or Albert Road—on the broad avenues of pounded brick bordered by palms and crotons and bougainvilleas and bamboos which made up the railway town of Ajaibpore. They had never seen the sea or a steamer; half their speech was helped out with native slang; they were all volunteers in the D.I.R.'s Railway Corps—grey with red facings—and their talk was exclusively about the Company and its affairs.

They all hoped to become engine-drivers earning six or eight hundred a year, and therefore they despised all mere sit-down clerks in the Store, Audit and Traffic departments, and ducked them when they met at the Company's swimming baths.

There were no strikes or tie-ups on the D.I.R. in those days, for the reason that the ten or twelve thousand natives and two or three thousand whites were doing their best to turn the Company's employment into a caste in which their sons and relatives would be sure of positions and pensions. Everything in India crystallizes into a caste sooner or later—the big jute and cotton mills, the leather harness and opium factories, the coal-mines and the dock-yards, and, in years to come, when India begins to be heard from as one of the manufacturing countries of the world, the labour Unions of other lands will learn something about the beauty of caste which will greatly interest them.

Those were the days when the D.I.R. decided that it would be cheaper to employ native drivers as much as possible, and the 'Sheds,' as they called the Repair Department, felt the change acutely; for a native driver could misuse his engine, they said, more curiously than any six monkeys. The Company had not then standardized its rolling-stock, and this was very good for apprentices anxious to learn about machines, because there were, perhaps, twenty types of locomotives in use on the road. They were Hawthornes; E types; O types; outside cylinders; Spaulding and Cushman double-enders and short-run Continental-built tank engines, and many others. But the native drivers burned them all out impartially, and the apprentices took to writing remarks in Bengali on the cabs of the repaired ones where the next driver would be sure to see them.

Young Ottley worked at first as little as the other apprentices, but his father, who was then a pensioned driver, taught him a great deal about the insides of locomotives; and Olaf Swanson, the red-headed Swede who ran the Government Mail, the big Thursday express, from Serai Rajgara to Guldee Haut, was a great friend of the Ottley family, and dined with them every Friday night.

Olaf was an important person, for besides being the best of the mail-drivers, he was Past Master of the big railway Masonic Lodge, 'St. Duncan's in the East,' Secretary of the Drivers' Provident Association, a Captain in the D.I.R. Volunteer Corps, and, which he thought much more of, an Author; for he had written a book in a language of his own which he insisted upon calling English, and had printed it at his own expense at the ticket-printing works.

Some of the copies were buff and green, and some were pinkish and blue, and some were yellow and brown; for Olaf did not believe in wasting money on high-class white paper. Wrapping-paper was good enough for him, and besides, he said the colours rested the eyes of the reader. It was called 'The Art of Road-Locos Repair or The Young Driver's Vademecome,' and was dedicated in verse to a man of the name of Swedenborg.

It covered every conceivable accident that could happen to an engine on the road; and gave a rough-and-ready remedy for each; but you had to understand Olaf's written English, as well as all the technical talk about engines, to make head or tail of it, and you had also to know personally every engine on the D.I.R., for the 'Vademecome' was full of what might be called 'locomotive allusions,' which concerned the D.I.R. only. Otherwise, it would, as some great locomotive designer once said, have been a classic and a text-book.

Olaf was immensely proud of it, and would pin young Ottley in a corner and make him learn whole pages—it was written all in questions and answers—by heart.

'Never mind what she *means*,' Olaf would shout. 'You learn her word-perfect, and she will help you in the Sheds. I drive the Mail—*the* mail of all India—and what I write and say is true.'

'But I do *not* wish to learn the book,' said young Ottley, who thought he saw quite enough of locomotives in business hours.

'You *shall* learn! I haf great friendship for your father, and so I shall teach you whether you like it or not.'

Young Ottley submitted, for he was really fond of old Olaf, and at the end of six months' teaching in Olaf's peculiar way began to see that the 'Vademecome' was a very valuable help in the repair sheds, when broken-down engines of a new type came in. Olaf gave him a copy bound in cartridge paper and hedged round the margins with square-headed manuscript notes, each line the result of years of experience and accidents.

'There is nothing in this book,' said Olaf, 'that I have not tried in my time, and I saw that the engine is like the body of a man. So long as there is steam—the life, you see—so long, if you know how, you can make her move a little—so!' He waggled his hand slowly. 'Till a man is dead, or the engine she is at the bottom of a river, you can do something with her. Remember that! *I* say it and I know.'

He repaid young Ottley's time and attention by using his influence to get him made a Sergeant in his Company, and young Ottley, being a keen Volunteer and a good shot, stood well with the D.I.R. in the matter of casual leave. When repairs were light in the Sheds and the honour of the D.I.R. was to be upheld at some far-away station against the men of Agra or Bandikui, the narrow-gauge railway-towns of the west, young Ottley would contrive to get away, and help to uphold it on the glaring dusty rifle-ranges of those parts.

A 'prentice never dreamed of paying for his ticket on any line in India, least of all when he was in uniform, and young Ottley was practically as free of the Indian railway system as any member of the Supreme Legislative Council who wore a golden General Pass on his watch-chain and could ride where he chose.

Late in September of his nineteenth year he went north on one of his cup-hunting excursions, elegantly and accurately dressed, with one-eighth of one inch of white collar showing above his grey uniform stock, and his Martini-Henry rifle polished to match his sergeant's sword in the rack above him.

The rains were out, and in Bengal that means a good deal to the railways; for the rain falls for three months lavishly, till the whole country is one sea, and the snakes take refuge on the embankment, and the racing floods puff out the brick ballast from under the iron ties, and leave the rails hanging in graceful loops. Then the trains run as they can, and the permanent-way inspectors spend their nights flourishing about in hand-carts pushed by coolies over the dislocated metals, and everybody is covered with the fire-red rash of prickly heat, and loses his temper.

Young Ottley was used to these things from birth. All he regretted was that his friends along the line were so draggled and dripping and sulky that they could not appreciate his gorgeousness; for he considered himself very consoling to behold when he cocked his helmet over one eye and puffed the rank smoke of native-made cigars through his nostrils. Until night fell he lay out on his bunk, in his shirt sleeves, reading the works of G.W.R. Reynolds, which were sold on all the railway bookstalls, and dozing at intervals.

Then he found they were changing engines at Guldee Haut, and old Rustomjee, a Parsee, was the new driver, with Number Forty in hand. Young Ottley took this opportunity to go forward and tell Rustomjee exactly what they thought of him in the Sheds, where the 'prentices had been repairing some of his carelessness in the way of a dropped crown-sheet, the result of inattention and bad stoking.

Rustomjee said he had bad luck with engines, and young Ottley went back to his carriage and slept. He was waked by a bang, a bump, and a jar, and saw on the opposite bunk a subaltern who was travelling north with a detachment of some twenty English soldiers.

'What's that?' said the subaltern.

'Rustomjee has blown her up, perhaps,' said young Ottley, and dropped out into the wet, the subaltern at his heels. They found Rustomjee sitting by the side of the line, nursing a scalded foot and crying aloud that he was a dead man, while the gunner-guard—who is a kind of extra-hand—looked respectfully at the roaring, hissing machine.

'What has happened?' said young Ottley, by the light of the gunner-guard's lantern.

'*Phut gya* [she has gone smash],' said Rustomjee, still hopping.

'Without doubt; but where?'

'*Khuda jahnta!* [God knows]. I am a poor man. Number Forty is broke.'

Young Ottley jumped into the cab and turned off all the steam he could find, for there was a good deal escaping. Then he took the lantern and dived under the drive-wheels, where he lay face up, investigating among spurts of hot water.

'Doocid plucky,' said the subaltern. '*I* shouldn't like to do that myself. What's gone wrong?'

'Cylinder-head blown off, coupler-rod twisted, and several more things. She is very badly wrecked. Oah, yes, she is a total wreck,' said young Ottley between the spokes of the right-hand driver.

'Awkward,' said the subaltern, turning up his coat-collar in the wet. 'What's to be done, then?'

Young Ottley came out, a rich black all over his grey uniform with the red facings, and drummed on his teeth with his finger nails, while the rain fell and the native passengers shouted questions and old Rustomjee told the gunner-guard to walk back six or seven miles and wire to someone for help.

'I cannot swim,' said the gunner-guard. 'Go and lie down.' And that, as you might say, settled that. Besides, as far as one could see by the light of the gunner-guard's lantern, all Bengal was flooded.

'Olaf Swanson will be at Serai Rajgara with the Mail. He will be particularly angry,' said young Ottley. Then he ducked under the engine again with a flare-lamp and sat cross-legged, considering things and wishing he had brought his 'Vademecome' in his valise.

Number Forty was an old reconstructed Mutiny engine,

with Frenchified cock-nosed cylinders and a profligate allowance of underpinning. She had been through the Sheds several times, and young Ottley, though he had never worked on her, had heard much about her, but nothing to her credit.

'You can lend me some men?' he said at last to the subaltern. 'Then I think we shall disconnect her this side, and perhaps, notwithstanding, she will move. We will try—eh?'

'Of course we will. Hi! Sergeant!' said the subaltern. 'Turn out the men here and do what this—this officer tells you.'

'Officer!' said one of the privates, under his breath. 'Didn't think I'd enlisted to serve under a Sergeant o' Volunteers. 'Ere's a 'orrible street accident. Looks like mother's tea-kettle broke. What d'yer expect us to do, Mister Civilian Sergeant?'

Young Ottley explained his plan of campaign while he was ravaging Rustomjee's tool-chest, and then the men crawled and knelt and levered and pushed and hauled and turned spanners under the engine, as young Ottley told them. What he wanted was to disconnect the right cylinder altogether, and get off a badly twisted coupler-rod. Practically Number Forty's right side was paralyzed, and they pulled away enough ironmongery there to build a culvert with.

Young Ottley remembered that the instructions for a case like this were all in the 'Vademecome,' but even he began to feel a little alarmed as he saw what came away from the engine and was stacked by the side of the line. After forty minutes of the hardest kind of work it seemed to him that everything movable was cleared out, and that he might venture to give her steam. She leaked and sweated and shook, but she moved—in a grinding sort of way—and the soldiers cheered.

Rustomjee flatly refused to help in anything so revolutionary as driving an engine on one cylinder, because, he said, Heaven had decreed that he should always be unlucky, even with sound machines. Moreover, as he pointed out, the pressure-gauge was jumping up and down like a bottle-imp. The stoker had long since gone away into the night; for he was a prudent man.

'Doocid queer thing altogether,' said the subaltern, 'but look here, if you like, I'll chuck on the coals and you can drive the old jigamaroo, if she'll go.'

'Perhaps she will blow up,' said the gunner-guard.

'Shouldn't at all wonder by the sound of her. Where's the shovel?' said the subaltern.

'Oah no. She's all raight according to my book, I think,' said young Ottley. 'Now we will go to Serai Rajgara—if she moves.'

She moved with long *ssghee! ssghee's!* of exhaustion and lamentation. She moved quite seven miles an hour, and—for the floods were all over the line—the staggering voyage began.

The subaltern stoked four shovels to the minute, spreading them thin, and Number Forty made noises like a dying cow, and young Ottley discovered that it was one thing to run a healthy switching-locomotive up and down the yards for fun when the head of the yard wasn't looking, and quite another to drive a very sick one over an unknown road in absolute darkness and tropic rain. But they felt their way along with their hearts in their mouths till they came to a distant signal, and whistled frugally, having no steam to spare.

'This *might* be Serai Rajgara,' said young Ottley, hopefully.

'Looks more like the Suez Canal,' said the subaltern. 'I say, when an engine kicks up that sort of a noise she's a little impatient, isn't she?'

'That sort of noise' was a full-powered, furious yelling whistle half a mile up the line.

'That is the Down Mail,' said young Ottley. 'We have delayed Olaf two hours and forty-five minutes. She must surely be in Serai Rajgara.'

"Don't wonder she wants to get out of it,' said the subaltern. 'Golly, what a country!'

The line here dipped bodily under water, and young Ottley sent the gunner-guard on to find the switch to let Number Forty into the siding. Then he followed and drew up with a doleful *wop! wop! wop!* by the side of the great forty-five-ton, six-wheel, coupled, eighteen-inch inside-cylinder Number Twenty-five, all paint and lacquer, standing roaring at the head of the Down Mail. The rest was all water—flat, level and solid from one point of the horizon to the other.

Olaf's red beard flared like a danger signal, and as soon as they were in range some knobby pieces of Giridih coal whizzed past young Ottley's head.

'Your friend very mad?' said the subaltern, ducking.

'Aah!' roared Olaf. 'This is the fifth time you make delay. Three hours' delay you make *me*—Swanson—the Mail! Now I will lose more time to break your head.' He swung on to the foot-board of Number Forty, with a shovel in one hand.

'Olaf!' cried young Ottley, and Olaf nearly tumbled backward. 'Rustomjee is behind.'

'Of course. He always is. But you? How you come here?'

'Oah, we smashed up. I have disconnected her and arrived here on one cylinder, by your book. We are only a—a diagram of an engine, I think.'

'My book! My very good book. My 'Vademecome'! Ottley, you are a fine driver. I forgive my delays. It was worth. Oh, my book, my book!' and Olaf leapt back to Number Twenty-five, shouting things about Swedenborg and steam.

'That is all right,' said young Ottley, 'but where is Serai Rajgara? We want assistance.'

'There is no Serai Rajgara. The water is two feet on the embankment, and the telegraph office is fell in. I will report at Purnool Road. Good-night, good boy!'

The Mail train splashed out into the dark, and Ottley made great haste to let off his steam and draw his fire. Number Forty had done enough for that night.

'Odd chap, that friend of yours,' said the subaltern, when Number Forty stood empty and disarmed in the gathering waters. 'What do we do now? Swim?'

'Oah, no! At ten-forty-five this morning that is coming, an engine will perhaps arrive from Purnool Road and take us north. Now we will lie down and go to sleep. You see there *is* no Serai Rajgara. You could get a cup of tea here once on a time.'

'Oh, my Aunt, what a country!' said the subaltern, as he followed Ottley to the carriage and lay down on the leather bunk.

For the next three weeks Olaf Swanson talked to everybody of nothing but his 'Vademecome' and young Ottley. What he said about his book does not matter, but the compliments of a mail-driver are things to be repeated, as they were, to people in high authority, the masters of many engines. So young Ottley was sent for, and he came from the Sheds buttoning his jacket and wondering which of his sins had been found out this time.

It was a loop line near Ajaibpore, where he could by no possibility come to harm. It was light but steady traffic, and a first-class superintendent was in charge; but it was a driver's billet and permanent after six months. As a new engine was on order for the loop, the foreman of the Sheds told young Ottley he might look through the stalls and sit himself.

He waited, boiling with impatience, till Olaf came in, and the two went off together, old Olaf clucking, 'Look! Look! Look!' like a hen, all down the Sheds, and they chose a nearly new Hawthorne, No. 239, which Olaf highly recommended. Then Olaf went away, to give young Ottley his chance to order her to the cleaning-pit, and jerk his thumb at the cleaner and say, as he turned magnificently on his heel, 'Thursday, eight o'clock. *Mallum?* Understand?'

That was almost the proudest moment of his life. The very proudest was when he pulled out of Atami Junction through the brick-field on the way to his loop, and passed the Down Mail, with Olaf in the cab.

They say in the Sheds that you could have heard Number Two hundred and Thirty-nine's whistle from Raneegunge clear to Calcutta.

Snow-Leopard

Flora Annie Steel

THE GUARD OF THE TRAIN STOOD
at the doorway of our first-class compartment apologetically. 'I
am afraid gentlemen,' he said, 'that you will have to wait for
your dinners. There has been a slight smash just up the line
and it may be the matter of an hour and a half before we can
get on.'

'And there isn't a restaurant car on the train,' I grumbled,
'just like England.'

The guard touched his hat and went forward with his tale
of woe. The only other occupant of the compartment, reached
up for his bundle of rugs, undid it, and spread one over his
knees; for dusk was on us, and it became cold in the high
Cumberland passes.

I literally gasped, for the rug in question was simply the
most beautiful snow-leopard skin I have ever seen, and it was
mounted *á distraction* on cream-coloured velvet embroidered in
gold and silver. Having hunted for many years in the Himalayas
I knew something about snow-leopards and I could not repress
the instant remark.

'What a splendid skin! May I ask if you shot it yourself?'

The owner, a man with dreamy eyes, replied absently, 'I did
not.' And I noticed that, as he spoke, he stroked the long silky
hair, so unlike that of a beast of prey, with the caressing touch
one would have given a favourite dog.

'Then if you bought it you must have paid a very long price for it,' I remarked again, for, as I have said, the skin was one in a thousand; possibly a million.

My fellow traveller smiled; a most attractive smile.

'I did not buy it either,' he replied, 'and it was not given to me—it came to me in a rather—I may say an extraordinary way. As we are here for—at any rate some little time—I will tell you the tale if you care to hear it.'

I jumped at the offer, and, settling himself comfortably with the wonderful rug well tucked round him, my fellow traveller began. He had a musical voice full of inflected cadences to which it was extremely pleasant to listen.

'It was a good many years ago when I was up in the wilds near Nepal. I was a bit of a climber and though I never attempted Everest—no one did in those days—I had managed a good many peaks. So, though it was a trifle late in the season, I determined on shortening my return to the plains by going over a col into the next valley. At the last moment, however, too much snow was reported for the baggage animals, so I started them early to do a roundabout by a forced march to my next camping ground, while I stopped behind to get a rare plant which I had located at the top of some rather inaccessible cliffs, and then, at my leisure, to go over the col by myself. The cliffs, however, proved more inaccessible than I had anticipated, and it was well afternoon before I started on my fifteen-mile trudge. As I have said, it was by no means difficult going, but the snow was very heavy quite obscuring tracks, and more than once I took a blind alley ending in hopeless glacier; for on both sides of the col there were peaks not over high but practically unclimbable at any rate without paraphernalia. The result being, that as the light began to fade, I began to wonder where I was exactly. If you are not a climber you will not understand what that means. It means that you start afresh. I was young and strong; so it was some time before any anxiety took hold of me, in fact I doubt if I ever was anxious. As I plodded on doggedly, the snow hardening as the cold increased, I admitted calmly that I had lost my way and that ere long I might have to dig myself in as a last chance. It was one of those moonless Indian nights when everyone of the millions

66

and millions of stars shines a different colour. All round me, save at my feet where the snow lay like a winding sheet, that glorious jewelled canopy! Precipices on either side of me; it was as if I were climbing to the very stars themselves. I must have fallen down some declivity or other, I think, for as I stumbled on, determined to do my best to the last, I saw dimly that I was in a sort of amphitheatre of high cliffs. Somewhere in them there might be a rift, a cave, some shelter.

'I believe I must have gone round those cliffs several times, becoming more and more dazed, more and more near the last till I could do no more. There was a recess. I might as well sleep the last sleep—if it was to be that—there as anywhere else. I staggered into it and leant against the sloping rock.

'And then strangely enough, I became aware that someone was singing, singing, singing. Then it couldn't be far from the end—the end of everything—not only love—Yes! It was Isolda singing. You could hear the marvellous accompaniment. Now it was Tristram's turn—Tristram must not be behind hand in the love duet—you see, I was something of a singer myself, and when one is near that long sleep, one dreams a bit. So Tristram broke in with the eternal cry of love.

'I may have sung it well, I may have sung it badly, I don't know. All of which I was conscious was a sudden blaze of light as something seemed to open in the cliff and a voice that said.

'"Who sings!"

'I was too far gone to answer. I stumbled forward to my knees, and found my hand clasped.

'Did I hear a voice say "Come in out of the cold?" I don't know. If I did it was my last conscious moment.

'When I came to myself it was quite a long time before I could realize where I was, in fact I don't realize it even now. It was a great big place full of light. Not sunlight; it was too white for that, but it cast shadows and it came from above. I judged the roof of the huge hall to be of glass—but again I don't know. One end of the place—call it cave, room, hall, what you will—was full of growing shrubs and flowers with birds and butterflies flitting about. I found out afterwards that this part was separated from the rest of the hall by a huge pane of glass—if it was glass. It looked as if it was, but it was quite pliant and rolled up as you would roll a window blind. So you see it mayn't have been glass. But everything was like that; familiar yet different.

'I was lying on a long chair and somebody was rubbing my feet. The hands that rubbed were warm and soft.

'Whose were they? I looked and looked at the figure in front of me, growing more and more confused: I suppose, really, that my brain had not begun to function properly. Finally I asked the question: 'Are you a boy or a girl?' that it was young was indubitable. A laugh echoed and echoed. It seemed to me as if that laugh must go on and on for ever.

'"I don't glue my hair and wear baggy trousers," said the voice, so I can't be a boy, and as I don't shingle or smoke or powder my nose, I can't be a girl—can I?"

'"Then what am I to call you?" I asked

'"Call me Homo!" came the reply, "and if you think it descriptive add 'Sapiens'."

'My stockings had been removed. Now a dry warm pair were being put on: but they were exactly the same pattern; cable-stitch—Lovat mixture—they were favourites of mine. My brain was still not functioning properly; for it left serious matters to intrigue itself with trifles. "But I thought my stockings would be soaked through," I said feebly.

'"That was very silly of you" came the answer "think them dry, and they are dry. It is only the mind that matters."

'I was too confused for philosophy: so I remained silent. What a face it was that looked into mine! At this distance of time I don't remember what it was like. I only know that it flahed like fire; that it seemed to hold all things by its sheer vitality.

'Once again what I am pleased to call my mind occupied itself with trivialities. "Didn't I hear the love duet in Tristram just now?"

'"You did. Would you like to hear it again? I'm afraid you will have to hold my hand if you do; for of course you haven't become a wireless receiver like I have."

'I felt my my hand clasped by a strong, soft, warm one and instantly the air was full of music.

'"Melba," I said weakly after a pause "and, and surely that is Jean-de-Reske, but I thought he was dead?"

'"What do you mean by dead?" was the quick question. '"Once sung always sung, you know. Ether waves and all that. Now if you want to hear anything else, you have only to put a name to it. Only please don't say the House of Commons. I can't stand that piffle."

'All this time a curious sense of well-being had been creeping over me. I seemed to have everything I wanted. You know it is not often that we human creatures feel absolutely content. Well, I did; but the odd thing was that I seemed to have everything I wanted, or ever could want, in myself.

'So I lay for a while lost in a dreamful laziness, while the figure opposite me sat on the floor, with those soft, warm, strong hands clasped over the crunched-up knees and its wonderful eyes so dark yet so full of light, fixed on mine. Then suddenly, as if in self-explanation I fulminated—

'"Evidently it is all electricity."

'My remark was countered by the query—

'"What is electricity?"

'And silence fell once more between us. I think it must have lasted some time, for I sat up suddenly, feeling vaguely that I had never felt better in my life. A desire to be up and doing possessed me; I looked at my companion with some pity. "Don't you find it lonely always living up here by yourself?" I asked.

'"I don't always live here" came the reply.

'"Then where—" I began.

'"Somewhere—anywhere—everywhere. And how can I feel lonely when the place is crammed full of people?"

'"People!" I echoed.

'There was a light laugh. "I forgot you don't understand television; but if you'll give me your hand once more, I think I can show you—not everything, mind you—but the outsides of things."

'And once again the strong, soft, warm clasp was mine. I saw instantly a miserable attic, bare of all things, even of a bed. On a heap of tumbled clothes in one corner lay a young man asleep. He looked hunger-stricken, but the expression on his face was content. He had evidently fallen asleep while reading, for a small book lay open beside him, his hand still marking the page. It was *Paradise Regained*.

"'He is a poet and makes nothing by his writing," came my companion's voice. "He often comes here; in fact at this moment he is sitting on the garden seat yonder listening to the birds, only you can't see him. You wouldn't, even if I were to roll up the non-conducting glass; for television is no use for the insides of things—you can see the outsides—that's all. And his outside isn't here. Now for another—."

'I became aware of a dimly lighted room—dimly lit yet still light and colourful and cheerful. An empty cot stood beside the bed. It was evidently a nursery. And on the bed, clasping tight in her hand a baby's shoe, lay a young woman who looked as if she had cried herself to sleep. But her face, also, was peaceful and content.

"'She is playing with her dead child on the rug yonder," said my companion quietly. "And so they all come——dozens of them. Then there are the other—who come from the other side, but television is no use there for they have no husks left for us to see. One can hear them sometimes, but one can't well tune up to an unknown wave length, can one?"

"'Then it *is* all electricity," I contended sleepily, for in good sooth my measureless content was making me drowsy.

"'What is electricity?" came the countering question again.

"'What is anything?" I re-countered feebly.

'Once again that echoing laugh seemed to fill the vast hall.

"'Imagination," replied Homo Sapiens with a smile that for glory beat all the sunrise and sunsets in the world. "Doesn't the soul lie in the imagination? Someone says that, somewhere. And now it's time we all went to bed. You'll be quite comfortable in that chair I expect, and here's a rug to keep you warm. The servants will bring you tea in the morning, and I'll take you downtown in my aeroplane after breakfast. Good-night. Don't be alarmed if you hear a noise. It is not the waifs, it is the music of the spheres. Don't let it disturb you."

'I caught a glimpse of a snow-leopard rug that glinted with gold and silver, and then came sudden darkness. It was less confusing than the light; but I had no time to wonder, no time even to realize the strangeness of the whole incident, the almost ludicrous co-mingling of early tea and television, knickerbocker stockings and imagination, for there stole upon my sense such sweet sounds that I lay entranced. Noise? Disturbance? Ye Gods. But this was music indeed. This held all things—No! It transcended all things, it rose and rose and rose carrying me with it.

'Whitherwards? Oh, Whitherwards? Whitherwards?—

'When I awoke the sun was streaming full on my face. But this was real sunlight. I sat up and looked round me. I had been lying on a perfect bed of maidenhair fern close to a little runnel of water. Behind me lay the snows, before me a cluster of hill huts which I recognized as the village to which I had been bound, but over me, keeping me warm, was this very leopard skin rug!

'How it got there—and indeed how I got there—I cannot say, even now. You in fact, are in precisely the same condition as I was, as I am now. The whole thing remains in my mind like some fantastic dream, though I am bound to confess I learnt, and am still learning, very much from it. I started to enquire, to experiment; but that is beside the question. Here as you see is the leopard skin rug. That at any rate is not imagination. For the rest, I questioned the villagers, and my servants who had arrived safely the night before. I re-climbed the snows, and searched for the amphitheatre of rocks. All to no avail. The most I could glean was a certain dread on the part of the villagers of the highest peak of the immediate range of snows, which was due apparently to a gigantic white bird that was said to be seen on moonlight nights hovering over it— most likely an aero . . . .

At this moment the door of the compartment was noisily pushed aside and a monstrous head all goggles and fur cap was thrust in.

'Oh! there you are old chap,' said a cheery voice. 'Got your wireless twenty minutes ago, and, as the missus didn't like keeping dinner waiting, I've brought the aero round waiting in the next field. Where are your duds?'

'Good for you,' cried my companion briskly.

The leopard skin rug was bundled up, a suitcase dragged

71

down from the rack, and with a brief 'Good-night, glad the tale was finished,' the dreamy-eyed man disappeared into the darkness.

A minute later I heard, very faintly, the hum of a rising plane.

I asked myself how the dickens the man had managed to send a wireless? Twenty minutes ago? Why, he had not left his seat . . . Was it possible . . . ?

The By-gone Days

Anonymous

A JOURNEY BY THE EASTERN
Bengal State Railway to-day is a care-free and comfortable one.
Every amenity that a railway company can provide for the
comfort and convenience of the traveller has been introduced
and the journey of 400 odd miles is finished in the waking
hours of the morning to the regret of many.

With the bridging of the Padma river the acceleration of the
train service has been possible and the northern terminus,
Siliguri, is reached at the comfortable hour of 6 a.m. It was not
always thus. While enjoying the comforts of modern travel, one
regrets the pleasant break in the journey to the foot of the
Himalayas, provided by the steamer service across the river
and dinner aboard ship. This, however, is the only regret.

Casting the mind back to the days when *khus-khus* tatties did
duty for electric fans and smelling, sometimes leaky castor oil
lamps shed a feeble light, the traveller felt thankful the journey
by the Eastern Bengal State Railway was performed in day
light, although the horrors of the night were still ahead in a
journey from Sara Ghat to Siliguri by the Northern Bengal State
Railway. That train service, the pioneer which prompted present
amenities, must have been designed with a purpose. It was an
absolute nightmare, nerve-racking and a severe strain on the
system. Noisy, bumpy and shaking in all directions, it plodded
its way toward the Himalayas, regardless of passengers'

comforts. It had to get there and it got there, though many parted with their dinner and their sleep—and then remained but fifty-two miles by the D.H. Railway, which had just cast off its original appellation of a steam railway to take on that of a railway. The journey over those fifty-two miles absolutely put in the shade the discomforts endured on the N.B.S.R.

Whereas the latter had shaken one in all directions, the convert did a sort of Charleston—an up and down movement—which still clings to it between Siliguri and Sukna. By the time travellers reached their destination they were pale and limp, and the commiseration of their friends on their enforced residence in the horrid plains fell on deaf ears.

They looked positively ill and done and when with the comforts of a fireside in house or hotel food was put in front of them, the horror of what they had endured in the past twenty-four hours brought forth a prompt head shake negating the idea of eating.

Darjeeling was reached at 4 p.m.

Things have changed for the very much better all round. The open trolleys on the wee railway have been replaced by comfortable carriages and electricity within recent years has in no small measure helped the avoidance of rushing into landslides which were not there on the downward journey.

But, even in those by-gone days people were thanking an all-wise Providence for the introduction of the railway, uncomfortable as it was, which had done away with a previous nightmare of travel—a journey from Calcutta to Bhagulpur and thence by boat to Karigola and the tonga service from Karigola to Pankhabari—the home of the palm-leaf fan, so greatly appreciated in the humid atmosphere of the Himalayan foothills a few hundred feet above the scorched up plains.

People are prone to grumble at all times, but when the mind goes back to those days, even though they were childhood's days, there seems to have been every reason for a grumble.

From Karigola to Titaliya, the military camping ground, sitting up in a tonga with the ear-piercing notes of the horn in one's ear most of the time, blown by the attendant to the driver even at the sight of a slinking jackal—there were tigers also by the way side in those days—generally brought a sigh of relief at the sight of the walls of the military cemetery ahead. It meant a rest, if not a pleasant halt, two miles up the road and an indifferent meal provided by the Titaliya dak bungalow khansama, who departed this life as an extensive landholder but his numerous charities, drawn from the pockets of tired and unsuspecting travellers, endure today giving him a *baranam* (bignam).

It was a restful break before repeating the experience in the last twenty-five miles that lay between Titaliya and Pankhabari *via* Maligara.

The indifferent food and the halt ahead put a different aspect on the last stage of the journey. The giant trees of the *swamp*, for this is the meaning of the word Terai, with orchids of many varieties hanging from their branches, the quaint thatch covered huts in the village of Mech or Bodo and Dhimal— aborigines—made a scene that still lies impressed on the mind. They have quaint customs. These aborigines of the Terai and of them much could be said, for since the nightmare of travel by *tonga* superseded by the horrors of a night journey by a newly constructed metre-gauge line, one had lived to see things undreamt of in one's philosophy, and chance directed I have journeyed to the land of Mech and Dhimal under pleasant circumstances undreamt of in the years I write of, and have lived and had my being with these quaint people all around me.

Times have indeed changed. The Pankhabari dak bungalow with its enviable visitor's book, containing names of men who made history and certainly made Darjeeling what it is today, has fallen under the hammer, leaving the old road up which one rode on diminutive ponies to Kurseong and thence by the old military road, *via* 'The Chimneys,' into Ghoom, abandoned and the haunt of unpleasant animals. The Terai tea planters' bazaar coolie alone treads the first half into Kurseong with chits for necessaries. He does other errands for the tea garden staff, but the nature of these errands is only relieved when he has looked upon the *rakshi*, provided at the Panighata grogshop, more than once.

Tea had been introduced in the Terai long prior to the introduction of the N.B.S.R., but with the coming of the railway there can be little doubt the industry received an impetus. The life of the tea planter in those days was a harum-scarum one, sort of sufficient for the day is the evil thereof. One day Messrs. Hurt and Feltwell and others journeyed down the line from Siliguri. They alighted at several stations inspecting tickets and giving advice *gratis* regarding changes of trains and the best means of arriving at Euston and Paddington.

At one station the train moved off with its usual jerk before Hurt and Feltwell had reached their own carriage. They made a rush for it, Feltwell got in all right but Hurt slipped and fell and but for Feltwell making a grab at him and dragging him bodily into the carriage, he would have been seriously injured, if not killed.

The station master noticing the accident stopped the train for enquiries of names and addresses. One asking Hurt his name, he replied, 'I am Hurt.' 'I know that sir,' said the station master, 'but what is your name?' 'I am Hurt.' 'My God, sir, I know that and will report accordingly, but I must have your name.' 'I am Hurt, I tell you.'

Turning to Feltwell in disgust, the poor station master enquired his name. 'I? Feltwell.' 'I know, sir, you are all right but the other gentleman is Hurt.' 'Quite, right, station master.'

The S.M. gave up. What he reported is not on record as these probably have been burnt long ago, but the fact remains that it cost these two planters Rs 25 each for breaking rules—boarding a train while in motion.

The Coolie

Anonymous

Hot platform, seething with humanity and flies. Fruit and sweet vendors plying their trades add to the general air of noisy confusion. Sleeping forms lying about are herded in every available patch of shade.

An incessant chorus of babbling mynas add to the din.

Trains, great fiery snorting monsters, forge their way from out of the heat haze and disgorge their cargo of passengers or goods.

Bare footed sweating coolies plunge into the melee. The sleeping figures, roused to activity, jostle and run with the rest.

Pandemonium reigns . . . . Packages are humped on straining backs . . . . Hoarse cries to clear the way . . . . And outside the tongawallahs seethe towards the station entrance in their eagerness to find a fare.

Nowhere is the scene without interest.

Slender women clutching brown babies follow, with a tinkle of anklets and bangles, in the wake of their husbands. Some are huddled in the voluminous folds of the disguising *burkha* lest alien eyes should gaze upon their charms. There, a fierce black bearded Hillman from the frontier; here, a Bengali babu complete with spectacles and umbrella. A demure child-wife, with soft shy eyes, passes with her veil half blown back from her frightened face—never before, perhaps, has she travelled and the bustle and roar bewilder her.

In the goodsyard coolies toil unceasingly. Wagons filled with sacks of grain or flour, bales of cotton, bundles of hide must all be unloaded. They work rhythmically to a monotonous chant. Muscles ripple beneath gleaming brown skins. For the most part they are happy. There are many worse things in life than being a coolie in regular employ.

One old man stands apart, and, with a hint of wistfulness in sunken eyes, watches the young men work. Days there were, when he, too, could labour as they.

What had it mattered when a wagon had been opened to reveal heavy piled up sacks? He had been wont to hurl himself upon them and, full of bursting energy, heave them one by one into the yard.

Those good days were gone.

His failing strength had been remarked upon—well he knew the head coolie to be his enemy. He had borne tales to the great ones—tales and lies, too, which told how the old coolie was lazy and also of how he would rip open a corner of a sack in order to steal a few handfuls of corn.

Of course the great ones had believed and he had been dismissed. He harboured no resentment for was it not ever thus?

Later, the head coolie had been found pilfering and he, also, had been sent away; the sahibs were ever just!

As yet the erstwhile coolie had not told his wife and growing family of the misfortune which had befallen. She was about to bear another child and women at such times must be protected. Each day her husband set out as though to work. Wearily, he would pad along the dusty highway—soon his few savings would be gone and what then? But they would last out until the child was born, and by that time, who knew, he might find work.

The old scene and the old life fascinated him, and so each day he came and stood apart, watching—ever watching.

The seeds of weakness were in his body, the lifting of a few more heavy loads and oblivion—his soul would speed away from his worn out body, he would dwell in the realms of the spirits of his forefathers. This must not be, for who would care for his house and family?

Thus, and ever thus, he pondered in his simple mind.

* * *

Each morning before the sun rose to full glory it was the custom of the memsahib to ride. The syce brought the little chestnut mare up to the steps and many a morning she shied away and lashed out dislodging a pot of ferns.

The memsahib laughed gaily and thought of the exhilarating gallop across the maidan.

'Have a care, old lady, I don't like the look in that animal's eye?'

Again the memsahib laughed and paid scant heed to the cautioning words of her husband. Springing lightly into the saddle she was out of the gate with a scurry of hoofs.

The syce shook his head and voiced his thoughts to the mali: 'That one has a heart of evil, she is no fit ride for the memlog!' And the wise mali agreed.

But the mare was going quietly now, the memsahib patted the arching neck. She loved her morning ride—no Indian liver for her, the warm blood coursed strongly through her veins.

Ahead was the funny old man whom she passed each day; always he salaamed her and smiled. She liked his old face, today she would speak to him.

'Ah, buddha, to where do you go each morning?' she called.

'Huzoor, I go to the railway station to work,' he lied, for he was the one-time coolie who had been dismissed.

'So? And the work is hard and the hours are long?'

'All work is good, memsahib!'

She laughed and carelessly flicked the pony with her whip. Maddened the chestnut mare reared, clawing the air with its forelegs, then it seized the bit between its teeth and dashed wildly down the road.

The memsahib was unprepared, she lost her head. The pony swerved, tried to jump a mud wall, blundered and fell, throwing its rider.

The memsahib lay stunned.

The coolie, very much afraid, ran to the spot.

'Memsahib—memsahib?' he called anxiously.

There was no movement from the prostrate figure. The memsahib's topee had fallen off and a blue bruise was darkening her forehead.

'Of a surety I shall be blamed for this!' muttered the coolie.

He would have liked to run away and hide but he could not leave her thus—besides she had smiled at him.

Wondering if it would kill him he stooped to hoist the unconscious girl on to his shoulders, just in the same way as he had carried the sacks of grain. He found her heavier than he expected.

With his burden he set off for the nearest bungalow. It was not far but his heart was throbbing curiously and his lungs did not seem to be working properly.

* * *

'Oh, I'm all right! It was only a knock on the head—what happened to the mare?'

Rather pale and shaken the memsahib was reassuring her distracted husband.

'Darling, are you sure you're all right? I shall have that brute shot!'

'No, no! It was all my fault—she's a topping ride. Please, Bobby, don't be silly! How did I get here, anyway?' she asked, looking round the strange bedroom.

'Oh, some old coolie carried you—thank God. These people are such fools, often they'd rather leave one to die.'

'Of course—I remember, I was talking to him. Where is he now?'

'I don't know. Hanging about for backsheesh, I suppose,' he said, ungratefully.

'He seemed a nice old man—works at the station,' she replied, while once again she visualized the rather wistful tired face.

It was decided that the memsahib could be moved back to her own bungalow by car. She felt giddy when she tried to walk and her husband put a steadying arm round her.

Outside the gate was a curled up, moaning figure. She recognized it.

'Stop! Stop!' she cried, 'that is the old man who brought me here! Oh! Bobby, he's hurt—we must do something!'

'All right, dear, I'll see to it later. Let me get you home first—.'

'No! We can't leave him like this!—Bobby?'

He could not withstand her pleading.

* * *

The old coolie was taken to the Mission Hospital.

He was hopelessly crocked—years of weight-lifting took their toll. He fought his way back to health and a semblance of his old self.

Once, the memsahib visited him. He was greatly touched by her solicitude.

'I am afraid you will never again be strong enough to work at the station,' she said, gently.

The old eyes dimmed.

'Preserver of the Poor,' he began, 'this unworthy one craves, forgiveness. Of my work at the station I spoke not the truth—.'

The whole pathetic little history came tumbling out, finishing with: 'Be not angry with thy servant!'

'I am not angry,' she replied, 'and I would help you. You risked your life for me, it is only right that I should reward you.'

The old man's eyes lit up with a gleam of hope—visions of his family starving had tortured his illness and retarded his recovery.

If only she could re-establish him at the station! A goodsyard chowkidar perhaps! The great white lords were all powerful— to be back on any sort of work at the station was the height of his ambition, and had he not been dismissed on a false charge?

Eagerly his eyes scanned her face. Would it be too much to ask?

She smiled. 'What would you that I should do for you?'

'Huzoor, even I, mean and humble as I am, have my pride. If of the memsahib's goodness a small position of trust at the station—such as chowkidar—could be found for me?' The voice trailed off uncertainly.

Anonymous

'I will see. If it is possible it shall be done.'

* * *

Now he walks proudly on his nightly rounds, guarding the sacks of grain that he was once supposed to have tampered with.

Many are the blessings which he calls down upon the head of the kind lady.

'Long may she prosper!'

And long may *he* prosper.

The Luck of John Fernandez

J.W. Best

ONCE CLEAR OF THE WESTERN
Ghats, it is to some people surprising that the traveller from
Bombay does not see more of the Indian jungles from the
windows of his comfortable railway carriage. Surprising, in
view of the enormous area of forest land that exists in peninsular
India; but not to be wondered at, however, when one grasps
the fact that railways must take the easy way through the level
plains whose wealth of grain and farm produce they tap.
Railways and forests have little use for one another. As
passengers, we naturally think of the lines solely from our own
point of view—speed and comfort. We forget that the carriage
of our mean bodies is an insignificant business compared with
the transport of heavy goods.

Once past the scrub clad slopes of the Western Ghats, which
are hardly worthy the name of jungle, the railways across the
Central Provinces hardly touch the forests. A patch at Bagra
on the Jubbulpur line, and another at Donragarh on the
Nagpur line, and that is all we see. So the traveller naturally
asks himself, Where are these jungles of which we read so
much?

Let him look from his carriage window across the rich crop
laden plains, over the fields of tall waving millet of white
speckled cotton, of pulses in ordered lines, or dark green
wheat, and he will see, often many miles away, the shapes of

distant blue hills on either side of the line. They overlook the sunny plains almost the whole way across the continent. Sometimes they are close enough for the passenger to see their base in detail, but more often only half their mass is visible above the line of the horizon. Perhaps the most outstanding of these hills is Dalla Pahar in the Bilaspur District, one of the most striking hills that I have ever seen, rising like a dark pyramid in the middle of a network of rice fields. As the train approaches, the tip of the hill first shows above the line of the distant horizon; soon the hill grows rapidly, so that when the carriages thunder over the Champa bridge Dalla Pahar stands like a dark sentinel brooding over the glaring plains.

In the long journey across the continent, those who know the hills watch them fascinated. These are the jungles of India, silent mountain tops, shaded valleys, and the deep foliage of the trees—what are their secrets?

Few indeed who penetrate the forests know what passes in their gloomy shelter. The deer are in the midst of plenty, but live, and feed, and breed, with swift death in their tracks. The heavy shouldered tiger, when his luck is out, so pressed for food that he must descend to a diet of frogs and crabs along the river beds; in more prosperous times he is so sated with food that half his kill is left to the bare-headed vultures and slinking hyaenas. Here roam the mighty bison, the dark skinned truculent boar and the clumsy bear.

As one looks across at these hills one can picture the brilliant peafowl, the screaming parrakeets, the furtive jungle fowl, the ungainly hornbill; and there is a great longing to be among them.

A small arm of the forest—rather, a little finger—crosses the railway for a short distance near Bagra. This you must picture to yourself, unless perchance you pass the place in the train as you read. Low forest, some bamboos, many thorns and deep shade beneath the shimmer of sun-kissed leaves above.

The name of Fernandez is as much honoured and is as well known in India as that of Jones or Evans in Wales. When I write of John Fernandez who worked as an engine driver on the railway at Itarsi in 1920, I am not referring to the one of that name that you know or knew. There may be fifty of them in Itarsi, they may all be engine drivers and they may all be known to their friends as John. Again I say that you do not know my John Fernandez and you will not find him in Itarsi. Did he ever exist? You ask. I am not going to give away either John or myself.

John was a good Catholic as well as a good father to his large family of children. He adored children, especially his own for whom he thanked God daily. John knew, like so many other fathers, that children need food and clothing, which cost money. John found it difficult to make both ends meet on his engine driver's pay in normal times. Now matters were worse with other calls on his purse. Moreover, Mrs Fernandez wanted to possess a gramophone.

Lent had been carefully observed in the Fernandez bungalow, and we find John at Easter much worried about finances. He spoke about it to the good Father, whom all loved—heathen, heretic, and Catholic alike—asking for advice.

'Father,' he said, 'Lent has saved my pocket. Now at Easter I should like to make a present to my wife, and to smell good roasted meat in the house again. I cannot afford the present, and it is going to be difficult to find the money for the house.'

'My son,' replied the Padre, 'put your trust in God and the intercession of St Anthony, remembering to take such opportunities as are sent you.'

John felt that the sum of fifty rupees would be wealth indeed if it could be come by honestly. But how? Miracles are scarce in these days—that sort of miracle, anyway.

The good Father had as firm a belief in prayer as a sound doctor has in castor oil. As an expert, the Padre had no hesitation in recommending St Anthony, who he knew to be a specialist in the particular kind of trouble that was affecting John. This is an age of specialists. The Padre had far more faith in St Anthony in his particular line of business than most doctors have in recommending their pet appendix snippers to their patients. John had a blind faith in the good Father—who indeed was a saint—and was therefore ready to put his shirt on St Anthony. So they both prayed. Of course prayer is not so fashionable as it was, but many folk still practise the healthy custom, which the Church of Rome is so old-fashioned as to encourage. She has not of course a monopoly in the virtue, but does set an example.

Their prayers were answered, as you will see if you have the patience to finish this story.

Some ten miles away from Itarsi, the railway crosses the sandy bed of the Tawa River by a bridge, then dives into a tunnel to emerge in that little finger of jungle that stretches over the line near Bagra. Here on the Railway line Fernandez found the answer to his prayers.

South of the railway, a short day's march distant, the Denwa River joins the Tawa. Here, where all is forest, dark rocks and overhanging bamboos shade the deep pools of clear water in the rivers. The further side of the stream is flat with rich alluvial soil on which grow many bér plum trees. At the time of which I write the grass beneath the trees had been closely cropped by game, leaving the many yellow plums that had fallen to the ground exposed to hungry eyes. A few large trees were scattered about which gave welcome shade where the sated animals could sit and chew the cud. The general effect was parklike and peaceful. The only sounds to be heard were the occasional whistle of a fruit pigeon as it piped its content in the higher branches of the trees, or the splash of a king-fisher probing the depths of the pool.

Beneath the shade of a green fig-tree, a sambur stag rested with legs tucked beneath his brown body. He had fed well on the luscious yellow plums; supplementing his diet with a salad of the fresh green *dhub* grass along the river bank. Now, with an occasional twitch of his large round ears, he sat in the shade watching the deep blue of the pool set like a jewel in the golden sand. His antlers, thickly beaded, heavy and dark, proclaimed him the father of his tribe. Every twenty seconds or so an upheaval in his stomach followed by a jerk in his throat would return the food to his mouth for the final meal. The stag took his time, chewing slowly as with half-closed eyes he watched the peaceful scene around him. In the deeper forest to his rear, the midday silence was rudely broken by the harsh call of a monkey. The stag stopped his rumination and slowly moved his ears as he tuned them to the direction of the warning call. Hearing the harsh cry of alarm repeated by many other monkeys, he rose, his antlers knocking noisily against a branch above him as he turned to face the danger, stamping his forelegs menacingly on the hard ground. What was it? A domestic affair in the monkey world? The bad dream of an ape? A false alarm at a wandering Jackal? The stag raised his head as he sniffed the still air. Ah! Dogs! Cruel red dogs, hungry and without mercy. Panic stricken, he turned from the foul stink of them towards the river sands splashing through the pool and clattering up the rocky slope on the other side of the water. The dogs, twelve couple of them, followed lean and hungry. The water boiled and hissed as they took it in the stag's wake. Then, silent footed, they followed their quarry whom they could hear crashing through the low growth on the ridge above them. They settled down to a steady hunt, certain of their prey. They followed at a dog's pace. The stag moved along in sudden rushes, each time prompted by the silent approach of the leader of the pack. His pursuers never hastened, being sure of their prey. Once the stag tried to break back, but was headed. Twice he attempted to make the sanctuary of the Tawa River on his left, each time only just escaping the cruel white fangs. After an hour of being hunted, the stag began to show distress. His flanks heaved and his eyes had a dazed look. Driven from his normal haunts, he was in strange forest where, for fear of man, beasts seldom venture. With thoughts only of the terror behind, the poor beast plunged on with the dogs closing in upon him as he struck the wire fencing of the railway line. Rising quickly he stood between the rails with bristling mane and fierce glaring eyes as he lowered his proud head for the charge. A dog ran in behind him. As the stag spun round he slipped on the slipper way and fell.

That same morning John Fernandez had made his Easter Communion; he was still feeling troubled about his finances while he made his way to the engine shed as he knew that he could not give his wife the gramophone that she wanted so badly, nor could there be a spread at dinner worthy the house of Fernandez. But he had not forgotten St Anthony, indeed the blessed saint's name resounded in his head to the throbs of the railway engine as he drove it eastwards. It seemed that the steam from the engine's bowels hissed the saint's name in regular throbs. 'Sssstán—on—y! sssssstán—tony! sssstán—tony!' it gasped as the train gained speed.

Time is a very worrying factor in the engine driver's life; he has to keep it, not lose it. John Fernandez had five comfortable minutes in hand as his train thundered over the Tawa bridge, disturbing the blue rock pigeons that circled between its piers. As the engine roared into the tunnel beyond, Fernandez looked ahead for daylight. Emerging, the train took the curve in the cutting, and as it did so, John saw in the straight ahead of him on the line, a confused mass of bushy tailed dogs scrambling over the carcass of a deer. I did not know if John wanted to put his brakes on. If he did it was of no use to try and stop the train in that short distance. I do know that the cowcatcher caught the body of the stag, hurling it back into the jungle down the embankment, at the same time raining red dogs on both sides of the line. Soon the brakes told, and the train pulled up. Telling his stoker to mind the engine. John Fernandez seized a heavy spanner and ran back along the line. Passing the guard he shouted to him to follow but the man was either too stupid or afraid to do so. With thanks to St Anthony, Fernandez rushed among such wounded dogs as still lived. The rest had fled from the appalling monster that smoked and hissed. John knew no fear; what he did know was that each dog's skin was worth fifteen rupees; so he smote and smote again with his heavy spanner. The good work finished, John wiped his brow with some cotton waste that he had in his pocket, then seizing two of the dogs by their tails, he dragged them to his engine where he stowed them away on the coal in the tender. Quickly backing his train, he piled up eight more of them. Then, after an anxious glance at his watch in which he realized that he had lost ten minutes of precious time, he marked the position of the dead stag and ran his train into Bagra station. Here he called upon a friend to help him unship the dead dogs for skinning, and arrange for the disposal of the venison left alongside the line. A frantic 'practice' telegram reached the good Father in Itarsi saying that St Anthony had done his work well.

By the time that the train had reached the end of its journey the time lost on account of the dogs had been made up—lost did I say! No; gained. The value of the skins presented for reward to Government was one hundred and fifty rupees. Allowing for acknowledgment to his various friends for help, Fernandez could safely rely on having a hundred rupees in his pocket, a good store of venison in his house, a sambur skin worth a few more rupees, and a trophy to adorn his home.

Was it wrong of John Fernandez to stop his train? Did he get into trouble over it? Ask the District Traffic Superintendent. He will probably tell you that I am a liar. Whatever he says about me I can survive it. I happen to know that the D.T.S. is a sportsman.

II

STORIES AFTER INDEPENDENCE

Loyalty

Jim Corbett

THE MAIL TRAIN WAS RUNNING AT its maximum speed of thirty miles per hour through country that was familiar. For mile upon mile the newly risen sun had been shining on fields where people were reaping the golden wheat, for it was the month of April and the train was passing through the Gangetic valley, the most fertile land in India. During the previous year India had witnessed one of her worst famines. I had seen whole villages existing on the bark of trees; on minute grass seeds swept up with infinite labour from scorching plains; and on the wild plums that grow on waste lands too poor for the raising of crops. Mercifully the weather had changed, good winter rains had brought back fertility to the land, and the people who had starved for a year were now eagerly reaping a good harvest. Early though the hour was, the scene was one of intense activity in which every individual of the community had his, or her, allotted part. The reaping was being done by women, most of them landless labourers who move from area to area, as the crop ripens, and who for their labour—which starts at dawn and ends when there is no longer light to work by—receive one-twelfth to one-sixteenth of the crop they cut in the course of the day.

There were no hedges to obstruct the view, and from the carriage window no mechanical device of any kind was to be seen. The ploughing had been done by oxen, two to a plough;

the reaping was being done by sickles with a curved blade eighteen inches long; the sheaves, tied with twisted stalks of wheat straw, were being carted to the threshing floor on ox-carts with wooden wheels; and on the threshing floor, plastered over with cow dung, oxen were treading out the corn; they were tied to a long rope, one end of which was made fast to a pole firmly fixed in the ground. As a field was cleared of the sheaves children drove cattle on to it to graze on the stubble, and amongst the cattle old and infirm women were sweeping the ground to recover any seed that had fallen from the ears when the wheat was being cut. Half of what these toilers collected would be taken by the owner of the field and the other half—which might amount to as much as a pound or two, if the ground was not too sun cracked—they would be permitted to retain.

My journey was to last for thirty-six hours. I had the carriage to myself, and the train would stop for breakfast, lunch, and dinner. Every mile of the country through which the train was running was interesting; and yet I was not happy, for in the steel trunk under my seat was a string bag containing two hundred rupees which did not belong to me.

Eighteen months previously I had taken employment as a Fuel Inspector with the railway on which I was now travelling. I had gone straight from school to this job, and for those eighteen months I had lived in the forest cutting five hundred thousand cubic feet of timber, to be used as fuel in locomotives. After the trees had been felled and billeted, each billet not more and not less than thirty-six inches long, the fuel was carted ten miles to the nearest point of the railway, where it was stacked and measured and then loaded into fuel trains and taken to the stations where it was needed. Those eighteen months alone in the forest had been strenuous, but I had kept fit and enjoyed the work. There was plenty of game in the forest in the way of chital, four-horned antelope, pig, and pea fowl, and in the river that formed one boundary of the forest there were several varieties of fish and many alligators and python. My work did not permit of my indulging in sport during daylight hours so I had to do all my shooting for the pot, and fishing, at night. Shooting by moonlight is very different from shooting in daylight, for though it is easier to stalk a deer or a rooting pig at night it is difficult to shoot accurately unless the moon can be got to shine on the foresight. The pea fowl had to be shot while they were roosting, and I am not ashamed to say that I occasionally indulged in this form of murder, for the only meat I ate during that year and a half was what I shot on moonlight nights; during the dark period of the moon I had perforce to be a vegetarian.

The felling of the forest disarranged the normal life of the jungle folk and left me with the care of many waifs and orphans, all of whom had to share my small tent with me. It was when I was a bit crowded with two broods of partridges—one black and the other grey, four pea fowl chicks, two leverets, and two baby four-horned antelope that could only just stand upright on their spindle legs, that Rex the python took up his quarters in the tent. I returned an hour after nightfall that day, and while I was feeding the four-footed inmates with milk I saw the lantern light glinting on something in a corner of the tent and on investigation found Rex coiled up on the straw used as a bed by the baby antelope. A hurried count revealed that none of the young inmates of the tent were missing, so I left Rex in the corner he had selected. For two months thereafter Rex left the tent each day to bask in the sun, returning to his corner at sundown, and during the whole of that period he never harmed any of the young life he shared the tent with.

Of all the waifs and orphans who were brought up in the tent, and who were returned to the forest as soon as they were able to fend for themselves, Tiddley-de-winks, a four-horned antelope, was the only one who refused to leave me. She followed me when I moved camp to be nearer to the railway line to supervise the loading of the fuel, and in doing so nearly lost her life. Having been brought up by hand she had no fear of human beings and the day after our move she approached a man who, thinking she was a wild animal, tried to kill her. When I returned to the tent that evening I found her lying near my camp bed and on picking her up saw that both her forelegs had been broken, and that the broken ends of the bones had worked through the skin. While I was getting a little milk down her throat, and trying to summon sufficient courage to

95

do what I knew should be done, my servant came into the tent with a man who admitted, to having tried to kill the poor beast. It appeared that this man had been working in his field when Tiddley-de-winks went up to him, and thinking she had strayed in from the nearby forest, he struck her with a stick and then chased her; and it was only when she entered my tent that he realized she was a tame animal. My servant had advised him to leave before I returned, but this the man had refused to do. When he had told his story he said he would return early next morning with a bone-setter from his village. There was nothing I could do for the injured animals, beyond making a soft bed for her and giving her milk at short intervals, and at daybreak next morning the man returned with the bone-setter. It is unwise in India to judge from appearances. The bone-setter was a feeble old man, exhibiting in his person and tattered dress every sign of poverty, but he was none the less a specialist, and a man of few words. He asked me to lift up the injured animal, stood looking at her for a few minutes, and then turned and left the tent, saying over his shoulder that he would be back in two hours. I had worked week in week out for months on end so I considered I was justified in taking a morning off, and before the old man returned I had cut a number of stakes in the nearby jungle and constructed a small pen in a corner of the tent. The man brought back with him a number of dry jute stalks from which the bark had been removed, a quantity of green paste, several young castor-oil plant leaves as big as plates, and a roll of thin jute twine. When I had seated myself on the edge of the camp bed with Tiddley-de-winks across my knees, her weight partly supported by her hind legs and partly by my knees, the old man sat down on the ground in front of her with his materials within reach.

The bones of both forelegs had been splintered midway between the knees and the tiny hooves, and the dangling portion of the legs had twisted round and round. Very gently the old man untwisted the legs, covered them from knee to hoof with a thick layer of green paste, laid strips of the castor-oil leaves over the paste to keep it in position, and over the leaves laid the jute stalks, binding them to the legs with jute twine. Next morning he returned with splints made of jute stalks strung together, and when they had been fitted to her legs Tiddley-de-winks was able to bend her knees and place her hooves, which extended an inch beyond the splints, on the ground.

The bone-setter's fee was one rupee, plus two annas for the ingredients he had put in the paste and the twine he had purchased in the bazaar, and not until the splints had been removed and the little antelope was able to skip about again would he accept either his fee or the little present I gratefully offered him.

My work, every day of which I had enjoyed, was over now and I was on my way to headquarters to render an account of the money I had spent and, I feared, to look for another job; for the locomotives had been converted to coal-burning and no more wood fuel would be needed. My books were all in perfect order and I had the feeling that I had rendered good service, for I had done in eighteen months what had been estimated to take two years. Yet I was uneasy, and the reason for my being so was the bag of money in my steel trunk.

I reached my destination, Samastipur, at 9 a.m. and after depositing my luggage in the waiting-room set out for the office of the head of the department I had been working for, with my account books and the bag containing the two hundred rupees. At the office I was told by a very imposing doorkeeper that the master was engaged, and that I would have to wait. It was hot in the open veranda, and as the minutes dragged by my nervousness increased, for an old railway hand who had helped me to make up my books had warned me that to submit balanced accounts and then admit, as I had every intention of doing, that I had two hundred rupees in excess would land me in very great trouble. Eventually the door opened and a very harassed-looking man emerged; and before the doorkeeper could close it, a voice from inside the room bellowed at me to come in. Ryles, the head of the Locomotive Department of the Bengal and North Western Railway, was a man weighing sixteen stone, with a voice that struck terror into all who served under him, and with a heart of gold. Bidding me sit down he drew my books towards him, summoned a clerk and very carefully checked my figures with those received from the stations to which the fuel had been sent. Then he told me he regretted my services would no longer be needed, said that discharge orders would be sent to me later in the day, and indicated that the interview was over. Having picked my hat off the floor I started to leave, but was called back and told I had forgotten to remove what appeared to be a bag of money that I had placed on the table. It was foolish of me to have thought I could just leave the two hundred rupees and walk away, but that was what I was trying to do when Ryles called me; so I went back to the table and told him that the money belonged to the railway, and as I did not know how to account for it in my books, I had brought it to him. 'Your books are balanced,' Ryles said, 'and if you have not faked your accounts I should like an explanation.' Tewari, the head clerk, had come into the room with a tray of papers and he stood behind Ryles' chair, with encouragement in his kindly old eyes, as I gave Ryles the following explanation.

When my work was nearing completion, fifteen cartmen, who had been engaged to cart fuel from the forest to the railway line, came to me one night and stated they had received an urgent summons to return to their village, to harvest the crops. The fuel they had carted was scattered over a wide area, and as it would take several days to stack and measure it they wanted me to make a rough calculation of the amount due to them, as it was essential for them to start on their journey that night. It was a dark night and quite impossible for me to calculate the cubic contents of the fuel, so I told them I would accept their figures. Two hours later they returned, and within a few minutes of paying them, I heard their carts creaking away into the night. They left no address with me, and several weeks later, when the fuel was stacked and measured, I found they had underestimated the amount due to them by two hundred rupees.

When I had told my story Ryles informed me that the Agent, Izat, was expected in Samastipur next day, and that he would leave him to deal with me.

Izat, Agent of three of the most flourishing railways in India, arrived next morning and at midday I received a summons to attend Ryles' office. Izat, a small dapper man with piercing eyes, was alone in the office when I entered it, and after complimenting me on having finished my job six months ahead of time, he said Ryles had shown him my books and given him a report and that he wanted to ask one question! Why had I not pocketed the two hundred rupees, and said nothing about it? My answer to this question was evidently satisfactory, for that evening, while waiting at the station in a state of uncertainty, I received two letters, one from Tewari thanking me for my contribution of two hundred rupees to the Railwaymen's Widows' and Orphans' Fund, of which he was Honorary Secretary, and the other from Izat informing me that my services were being retained, and instructing me to report to Ryles for duty.

For a year thereafter I worked up and down the railway on a variety of jobs, at times on the footplates of locomotives reporting on consumption of coal—a job I liked for I was permitted to drive the engines; at times as guard of goods trains, a tedious job, for the railway was short-handed and on many occasions I was on duty for forty-eight hours at a stretch; and at times as assistant storekeeper, or assistant station-master. And then one day I received orders to go to Mokameh Ghat and see Storrar, the Ferry Superintendent. The Bengal and North Western Railway runs through the Gangetic-valley at varying distances from the Ganges river, and at several places branch lines take off from the main line and run down to the river and, by means of ferries, connect up with the broad-gauge railways on the right bank. Mokameh Ghat on the right bank of the Ganges is the most important of these connections.

I left Samastipur in the early hours of the morning and at the branch-line terminus, Samaria Ghat, boarded the S.S. Gorakhpur. Storrar had been apprised of my visit but no reason had been given, and as I had not been told why I was to go to Mokameh Ghat, we spent the day partly in his house and partly in walking about the extensive sheds, in which there appeared to be a considerable congestion of goods. Two days later I was summoned to Gorakhpur, the headquarters of the railway, and informed that I had been posted to Mokameh Ghat as Trans-shipment Inspector, that my pay had been increased from one hundred to one hundred and fifty rupees per month, and that I was to take over the contract for handling goods a week later.

So back to Mokameh Ghat I went, arriving on this occasion at night, to take up a job about which I knew nothing, and to take on a contract without knowing where to get a single labourer, and, most important of all, with a capital of only one hundred and fifty rupees, saved during my two and a half years' service.

Storrar was not expecting me on this occasion, but he gave me dinner, and when I told him why I had returned we took our chairs on to the veranda, where a cool wind was blowing off the river, and talked late into the night. Storrar was twice my age and had been at Mokameh Ghat for several years. He was employed as Ferry Superintendent by the Bengal and North Western (metre-gauge) Railway, and was in charge of a fleet of steamers and barges that ferried passengers and metre-gauge wagons between Samaria Ghat and Mokameh Ghat. I learnt from him that eighty per cent of the long-distance traffic on the Bengal and North Western Railway passed through Mokameh Ghat; and that each year, from March to September, congestion of goods traffic took place at Mokameh Ghat and caused serious loss to the Railway.

The transfer of goods between the two railways at Mokameh Ghat, necessitated by a break of gauge, was done by a Labour Company which held the contract for handling goods throughout the length of the broad-gauge railway. In Storrar's opinion the indifference of this company to the interests of the metre-gauge railway, and the seasonal shortage of labour due to the harvesting of crops in the Gangetic valley, were the causes of the annual congestion. Having imparted this information, he very pertinently asked how I, a total stranger to the locality and without any capital—he brushed aside my hard-earned savings—proposed to accomplish what the Labour Company with all their resources had failed to do. The sheds at Mokameh Ghat, he added, were stacked to the roof with goods, there were four hundred wagons in the yard waiting to be unloaded, and a thousand wagons on the far side of the river waiting to be ferried across. 'My advice to you,' he concluded, 'is to catch the early steamer to Samaria Ghat and to go straight back to

Gorakhpur. Tell the railway you will have nothing to do with the handling contract.'

I was up early next morning but I did not catch the steamer to Samaria Ghat. Instead, I went on a tour of inspection of the sheds and of the goods yard. Storrar had not overpainted the picture: in fact the conditions were even worse than he had said they were, for in addition to the four hundred metre-gauge wagons there were the same number of broad-gauge wagons waiting to be unloaded. At a rough calculation I put the goods at Mokameh Ghat waiting to be dealt with at fifteen thousand tons, and I had been sent to clear up the mess. Well, I was not quite twenty-one years of age, and summer was starting, a season when all of us are a little bit mad. By the time I met Ram Saran I had made up my mind that I would take on the job, no matter what the result might be.

Ram Saran was station-master at Mokameh Ghat, a post he had held for two years. He was twenty years older than I was, had an enormous jet black beard, and was the father of five children. He had been advised by telegram of my arrival, but had not been told that I was to take over the handling contract. When I gave him this bit of news his face beamed all over and he said, 'Good, sir. Very good. We will manage.' My heart warmed towards Ram Saran on hearing that 'we', and up to his death, thirty-five years later, it never cooled.

When I told Storrar over breakfast that morning that I had decided to take on the handling contract he remarked that fools never took good advice, but added that he would do all he could to help me, a promise he faithfully kept. In the months that followed he kept his ferry running day and night to keep me supplied with wagons.

The journey from Gorakhpur had taken two days, so when I arrived at Mokameh Ghat I had five days in which to learn what my duties were, and to make arrangements for taking over the handling contract. The first two days I spent in getting acquainted with my staff which, in addition to Ram Saran, consisted of an assistant station-master, a grand old man by the name of Chatterji who was old enough to be my grandfather, sixty-five clerks, and a hundred shunters, pointsmen, and watchmen. My duties extended across the river to Samaria

Ghat where I had a clerical and menial staff a hundred strong. The supervising of these two staffs, and the care of the goods in transit, was in itself a terrifying job and added to it was the responsibility of providing a labour force sufficient to keep the five hundred thousand tons of goods that passed through Mokameh Ghat annually flowing smoothly.

The men employed by the big Labour Company were on piece work, and as all work at Mokameh Ghat was practically at a standstill, there were several hundred very discontented men sitting about the sheds, many of whom offered me their services when they heard that I was going to do the handling for the metre-gauge railway. I was under no agreement not to employ the Labour Company's men, but thought it prudent not to do so. However, I saw no reason why I should not employ their relatives, so on the first of the three days I had in hand I selected twelve men and appointed them headmen. Eleven of these headmen undertook to provide ten men each, to start with, for the handling of goods, and the twelfth undertook to provide a mixed gang of sixty men and women for the handling of coal. The traffic to be dealt with consisted of a variety of commodities, and this meant employing different castes to deal with the different classes of goods. So of the twelve headmen, eight were Hindus, two Mohammedans, and two men of the depressed class; and as only one of the twelve was literate I employed one Hindu and one Mohammedan clerk to keep their accounts.

While one Labour Company was doing the work of both railways the interchange of goods had taken place from wagon to wagon. Now each railway was to unload its goods in the sheds, and reload from shed to wagon. For all classes of goods, excluding heavy machinery and coal, I was to be paid at the rate of Re 1-7-0 (equivalent to 1*s*. 11*d*. at the rate of exchange then current) for every thousand maunds of goods unloaded from wagons to shed or loaded from shed to wagons. Heavy machinery and coal were one-way traffic and as these two commodities were to be trans-shipped from wagon to wagon and only one contractor could be employed for the purpose, the work was entrusted to me, and I was to receive Re 1-4-0 (1*s*. 8*d*.) for unloading, and the same for loading, one thousand maunds. There are eighty pounds in a maund, and a thousand maunds therefore are equal to over thirty-five tons. These rates will appear incredible, but their accuracy can be verified by a reference to the records of the two railways.

A call-over on the last evening revealed that I had eleven headmen, each with a gang of ten men, and one headman with a mixed gang of sixty men and women. This, together with the two clerks, completed my force. At day-break next morning I telegraphed to Gorakhpur that I had assumed my duties as trans-shipment Inspector, and had taken over the handling contract.

Ram Saran's opposite number on the broad-gauge railway was an Irishman by the name of Tom Kelly. Kelly had been at Mokameh Ghat for some years and though he was very pessimistic of my success, he very sportingly offered to help me in every way he could. With the sheds congested with goods, and with four hundred wagons of each railway waiting to be unloaded, it was necessary to do something drastic to make room in the sheds and get the traffic moving, so I arranged with Kelly that I would take the risk of unloading a thousand tons of wheat on the ground outside the sheds and with the wagons so released clear a space in the sheds for Kelly to unload a thousand tons of salt and sugar. Kelly then with his empty wagons would clear a space in the sheds for me. This plan worked admirably. Fortunately for me it did not rain while my thousand tons of wheat were exposed to the weather, and in ten days we had not only cleared the accumulation in the sheds but also the accumulation of wagons. Kelly and I were then able to advise our respective headquarters to resume the booking of goods via Mokameh Ghat, which had been suspended for a fortnight.

I took over the contract at the beginning of the summer, the season when traffic on Indian railways is at its heaviest, and as soon as booking was opened a steady stream of downwards traffic from the Bengal and North Western Railway and an equally heavy stream from the broad-gauge railway started pouring into Mokameh Ghat. The rates on which I had been given the contract were the lowest paid to any contractor in India, and the only way in which I could hope to keep my labour was by cutting it down to the absolute minimum and making it work harder in order that it would earn as much, or possibly a little more, than other labour on similar work. All the labour at Mokameh Ghat was on piece work, and at the end of the first week my men and I were overjoyed to find that they had earned, on paper, fifty per cent more than the Labour Company's men had earned.

When entrusting me with the contract the railway promised to pay me weekly, and I on my part promised to pay my labour weekly. The railway, however, when making their promise, failed to realize that by switching over from one handling contractor to another they would be raising complications for their Audit Department that would take time to resolve. For the railway this was a small matter, but for me it was very different. My total capital on arrival at Mokameh Ghat had been one hundred and fifty rupees, and there was no one in all the world I could call on to help me with a loan, so until the railway paid me I could not pay my men.

I have entitled this story 'Loyalty', and I do not think that anyone has ever received greater loyalty than I did, not only from my labour, but also from the railway staff, during those first three months that I was at Mokameh Ghat. Nor do I think that men have ever worked harder. The work started every morning, weekdays and Sundays alike, at 4 a.m., and continued without interruption up to 8 p.m. The clerks whose duty it was to check and tally the goods took their meals at different hours to avoid a stoppage of work and my men ate their food, which was brought to them by wives, mothers, or daughters, in the sheds. There were no trade unions or slaves and slave-drivers in those days and every individual was at liberty to work as many, or as few, hours as he or she wished to. And everyone worked cheerfully and happily; for no matter whether it was the procuring of more and better food and clothing for the family, the buying of a new ox to replace a worn-out one, or the paying-off of a debt, the incentive, without which no man can work his best, was there. My work and Ram Saran's did not end when the men knocked off work, for there was correspondence to attend to, and the next day's work to be planned and arranged for, and during those first three months neither of us spent more than four hours in bed each night. I was not twenty-one and as hard as nails, but Ram Saran was twenty years older and soft, and at the end of the three months he had lost a stone in weight but none of his cheerfulness.

Lack of money was now a constant worry to me, and as week succeeded week the worry became a hideous nightmare that never left me. First the headmen and then the labourers pledged their cheap and pitiful bits of jewellery and now all credit had gone; and to make matters worse, the men of the Labour Company, who were jealous that my men had earned more than they did, were beginning to taunt my men. On several occasions ugly incidents were narrowly avoided, for semi-starvation had not impaired the loyalty of my men and they were willing to give battle to anyone who as much as hinted that I had tricked them into working for me, and that they would never see a piece of the money they had earned.

The monsoon was late in coming that year and the red ball in the sky, fanned by a wind from an unseen furnace, was making life a burden. At the end of a long and a very trying day I received a telegram from Camaria Ghat informing me that an engine had been derailed on the slipway that fed the barges on which wagons were ferried across to Mokameh Ghat. A launch conveyed me across the river and twice within the next three hours the engine was replaced on the track, with the aid of hand jacks, only to be derailed again. It was not until the wind had died down and the powdery sand could be packed under the wooden sleepers that the engine was re-railed for the third time, and the slipway again brought into use. Tired and worn out, and with eyes swollen and sore from the wind and sand, I had just sat down to my first meal that day when my twelve headmen filed into the room, and seeing my servant placing a plate in front of me, with the innate courtesy of Indians, filed out again. I then, as I ate my dinner, heard the following conversation taking place in the veranda.

One of the headmen: What was on the plate you put in front of the sahib?

My servant: A chapati and a little dal.

One of the headmen: Why only one chapati and a little dal?

My servant: Because there is no money to buy more.

One of the headmen: What else does the sahib eat?

My servant: Nothing.

After a short silence I heard the oldest of the headmen, a Mohammedan with a great beard dyed with henna, say to his companions, 'Go home. I will stay and speak to the sahib.'

When my servant had removed the empty plate the old headman requested permission to enter the room, and standing before me spoke as follows: 'We came to tell you that our stomachs have long been empty and that after tomorrow it would be no longer possible for us to work. But we have seen tonight that your case is as bad as ours and we will carry on as long as we have strength to stand. I will, with your permission, go now, sahib, and for the sake of Allah, I beg you will do something to help us.'

Every day for weeks I had been appealing to head-quarters at Gorakhpur for funds and the only reply I could elicit was that steps were being taken to make early payment of my bills.

After the bearded headman left me that night I walked across to the Telegraph Office, where the telegraphist on duty was sending the report I submitted each night of the work done during the day, took a form off his table and told him to clear the line for an urgent message to Gorakhpur. It was then a few minutes after midnight and the message I sent read: 'Work at Mokameh Ghat ceases at midday today unless I am assured that twelve thousand rupees has been dispatched by morning train.' The telegraphist read the message over and looking up at me said: 'If I have your permission I will tell my brother, who is on duty at this hour, to deliver the message at once and not wait until office hours in the morning. Ten hours later, and with two hours of my ultimatum still to run, I saw a telegraph messenger hurrying towards me with a buff-coloured envelope in his hand. Each group of men he passed stopped work to stare after him, for everyone in Mokameh Ghat knew the purport of the telegram I had sent at midnight. After I had read the telegram the messenger, who was the son of my office peon, asked if the news was good; and when I told him it was good, he dashed off and his passage down the sheds was punctuated by shouts of delight. The money could not arrive until the following morning, but what did a few hours matter to those who had waited for long months?

The pay clerk who presented himself at my office next day, accompanied by some of my men carrying a cash chest slung on a bamboo pole and guarded by two policemen, was a jovial Hindu who was as broad as he was long and who exuded good humour and sweat in equal proportions. I never saw him without a pair of spectacles tied across his forehead with red tape. Having settled himself on the floor of my office he drew on a cord tied round his neck and from somewhere deep down in his person pulled up a key. He opened the cash chest, and lifted out twelve string-bags each containing one thousand freshly minted silver rupees. He licked a stamp, and stuck it to the receipt I had signed. Then, delving into a pocket that would comfortably have housed two rabbits, he produced an envelope containing bank notes to the value of four hundred and fifty rupees, my arrears of pay for three months.

I do not think anyone has ever had as great pleasure in paying out money as I had when I placed a bag containing a thousand rupees into the hands of each of the twelve headmen, nor do I think men have ever received money with greater pleasure than they did. The advent of the fat pay clerk had relieved a tension that had become almost unbearable, and the occasion called for some form of celebration, so the remainder of the day was declared a holiday—the first my men and I had indulged in for ninety-five days. I do not know how the others spent their hours of relaxation. For myself, I am not ashamed to admit that I spent mine in sound and restful sleep.

For twenty-one years my men and I worked the handling contract at Mokameh Ghat, and during the whole of that long period, and even when I was absent in France and in Waziristan during the 1914–18 war, the traffic flowed smoothly through the main outlet of the Bengal and North Western Railway with never a hitch. When we took over the contract, between four and five hundred thousand tons of goods were passing through Mokameh Ghat, and when I handed over to Ram Saran the traffic had increased to a million tons.

Those who visit India for pleasure or profit never come in contact with the real Indian—the Indian whose loyalty and

107

devotion alone made it possible for a handful of men to administer, for close on two hundred years, a vast subcontinent with its teeming millions. To impartial historians I will leave the task of recording whether or not that administration was beneficial to those to whom I have introduced you, the poor of my India.

Mano Majra Station

Khushwant Singh

Early in September the time
schedule in Mano Majra started going wrong. Trains became
less punctual than ever before and many more started to run
through at night. Some days it seemed as though the alarm
clock had been set for the wrong hour. On others, it was as if
no one had remembered to wind it. Imam Baksh waited for
Meet Singh to make the first start. Meet Singh waited for the
mullah's call to prayer before getting up. People stayed in bed
late without realizing that times had changed and the mail
train might not run through at all. Children did not know
when to be hungry, and clamoured for food all the time. In the
evenings, everyone was indoors before sunset and in bed before
the express came by—if it did come by. Goods trains had
stopped running altogether, so there was no lullaby to lull
them to sleep. Instead, ghost trains went past at odd hours
between midnight and dawn, disturbing the dreams of Mano
Majra.

This was not all that changed the life of the village. A unit
of Sikh soldiers arrived and put up tents near the railway
station. They built a six-foot-high square of sandbags about the
base of the signal near the bridge, and mounted a machine gun
in each face. Armed sentries began to patrol the platform and
no villagers were allowed near the railings. All trains coming
from Delhi stopped and changed their drivers and guards

before moving on to Pakistan. Those coming from Pakistan ran through with their engines screaming with release and relief.

One morning, a train from Pakistan halted at Mano Majra railway station. At first glance, it had the look of the trains in the days of peace. No one sat on the roof. No one clung between the bogies. No one was balanced on the footboards. But somehow it was different. There was something uneasy about it. It had a ghostly quality. As soon as it pulled up to the platform, the guard emerged from the tail end of the train and went into the station-master's office. Then the two went to the soldiers' tents and spoke to the officer in charge. The soldiers were called out and the villagers loitering about were ordered back to Mano Majra. One man was sent off on a motorcycle to Chundunnugger. An hour later, the sub-inspector with about fifty armed policemen turned up at the station. Immediately after them, Mr Hukum Chand drove up in his American car.

The arrival of the ghost train in broad daylight created a commotion in Mano Majra. People stood on their roofs to see what was happening at the station. All they could see was the black top of the train stretching from one end of the platform to the other. The station building and the railings blocked the rest of the train from view. Occasionally a soldier or a policeman came out of the station and then went back again.

In the afternoon, men gathered in little groups, discussing the train. The groups merged with each other under the peepul tree, and then everyone went into the gurdwara. Women, who had gone from door to door collecting and dropping bits of gossip, assembled in the headman's house and waited for their menfolk to come home and tell them what they had learned about the train.

This was the pattern of things at Mano Majra when anything of consequence happened. The women went to the headman's house, the men to the temple. There was no recognized leader of the village. Banta Singh, the headman, was really only a collector of revenue—a lambardar. The post had been in his family for several generations. He did not own any more land than the others. Nor was he a head in any other way. He had no airs about him: he was a modest hard-working peasant like the rest of his fellow villagers. But since government officials and the police dealt with him, he had an official status. Nobody called him by his name. He was 'O Lambardara,' as his father, his father's father, and his father's father's father had been before him.

The only men who voiced their opinions at village meetings were Imam Baksh, the mullah of the mosque, and Bhai Meet Singh. Imam Baksh was a weaver, and weavers are traditionally the butt of jokes in the Punjab. They are considered effeminate and cowardly—a race of cuckolds whose women are always having liaisons with others. But Imam Baksh's age and piety had made him respected. A series of tragedies in his family had made him an object of pity, and then of affection. The Punjabis love people they can pity. His wife and only son had died within a few days of each other. His eyes, which had never been very good, suddenly became worse and he could not work his looms any more. He was reduced to beggary, with a baby girl, Nooran, to look after. He began living in the mosque and teaching Muslim children the Koran. He wrote out verses from the Koran for the village folk to wear as charms or for the sick to swallow as medicine. Small offerings of flour, vegetables, food, and cast-off clothes kept him and his daughter alive. He had an amazing fund of anecdotes and proverbs which the peasants loved to hear. His appearance commanded respect. He was a tall, lean man, bald save for a line of white hair which ran round the back of his head from ear to ear, and he had a neatly trimmed silky white beard that he occasionally dyed with henna to a deep orange-red. The cataract in his eyes gave them a misty philosophical look. Despite his sixty years, he held himself erect. All this gave his bearing a dignity and an aura of righteousness. He was known to the villagers not as Imam Baksh or the mullah but as Chacha, or Uncle.

Meet Singh inspired no such affection and respect. He was only a peasant who had taken to religion as an escape from work. He had a little land of his own which he had leased out, and this, with the offerings at the temple, gave him a comfortable living. He had no wife or children. He was not learned in the scriptures, nor had he any faculty for conversation. Even his appearance was against him. He was short, fat, and hairy. He

111

was the same age as Imam Baksh, but his beard had none of
the serenity of the other's. It was black, with streaks of grey.
And he was untidy. He wore his turban only when reading the
scripture. Otherwise, he went about with his long hair tied in
a loose knot held by a little wooden comb. Almost half of the
hair was scattered on the nape of his neck. He seldom wore a
shirt and his only garment—a pair of shorts—was always
greasy with dirt. But Meet Singh was a man of peace. Envy had
never poisoned his affection for Imam Baksh. He only felt that
he owed it to his own community to say something when
Imam Baksh made any suggestions. Their conversation always
had an undercurrent of friendly rivalry.

The meeting in the gurdwara had a melancholic atmosphere.
People had little to say, and those who did spoke slowly, like
prophets.

Imam Baksh opened the discussion. 'May Allah be merciful.
We are living in bad times.'

A few people sighed solemnly, 'Yes, bad days.'

Meet Singh added, 'Yes, Chacha—this is Kalyug, the dark
age.'

There was a long silence and people shuffled uneasily on
their haunches. Some yawned, closing their mouths with loud
invocations to God: 'Ya Allah. Wah Guru, wah Guru.'

'Lambardara,' started Imam Baksh again, 'you should know
what is happening. Why has not the Deputy Sahib sent for
you?'

'How am I to know, Chacha? When he sends for me I will
go. He is also at the station and no one is allowed near it.'

A young villager interjected in a loud cheery voice: 'We are
not going to die just yet. We will soon know what is going on.
It is a train after all. It may be carrying government treasures
or arms. So they guard it. Haven't you heard, many have been
looted?'

'Shut up,' rebuked his bearded father angrily. 'Where there
are elders, what need have you to talk?'

'I only . . . .'

'That is all,' said the father sternly. No one spoke for some
time.

'I have heard,' said Imam Baksh, slowly combing his beard

with his fingers, 'that there have been many incidents with trains.'

The word 'incident' aroused an uneasy feeling in the audience. 'Yes, lots of incidents have been heard of,' Meet Singh agreed after a while.

'We only ask for Allah's mercy,' said Imam Baksh, closing the subject he had himself opened.

Meet Singh, not meaning to be outdone in the invocation to God, added, 'Wah Guru, wah Guru.'

They sat on in a silence punctuated by yawns and murmurs of 'Ya Allah' and 'Hey wah Guru'. Several people, on the outer fringe of the assembly, stretched themselves on the floor and went to sleep.

Suddenly a policeman appeared in the doorway of the gurdwara. The lambardar and three or four villagers stood up. People who were asleep were prodded into getting up. Those who had been dozing sat up in a daze, exclaiming, 'What is it? What's up?' Then hurriedly wrapped their turbans round their heads.

'Who is the lambardar of the village?'

Banta Singh walked up to the door. The policeman took him aside and whispered something. Then as Banta Singh turned back, he said loudly: 'Quickly, within half an hour. There are two military trucks waiting on the station side. I will be there.'

The policeman walked away briskly.

The villagers crowded round Banta Singh. The possession of a secret had lent him an air of importance. His voice had a tone of authority.

'Everyone get all the wood there is in his house and all the kerosene oil he can spare and bring these to the motor trucks on the station side. You will be paid.'

The villagers waited for him to tell them why. He ordered them off brusquely. 'Are you deaf? Haven't you heard? Or do you want the police to whip your buttocks before you move? Come along quickly.'

People dispersed into the village lanes whispering to each other. The lambardar went to his own house.

A few minutes later, villagers with bundles of wood and bottles of oil started assembling outside the village on the

113

station side. Two large mud-green army trucks were parked alongside each other. A row of empty petrol cans stood against a mud well. A Sikh soldier with a sten gun stood on guard. Another Sikh, an officer with his beard neatly rolled in a hair net, sat on the back of one of the trucks with his feet dangling. He watched the wood being stacked in the other truck and nodded his head in reply to the villagers' greetings. The lambardar stood beside him, taking down the names of the villagers and the quantities they brought. After dumping their bundles of wood on the truck and emptying bottles of kerosene into the petrol cans, the villagers collected in a little group at a respectful distance from the officer.

Imam Baksh put down on the truck the wood he had carried on his head and handed his bottle of oil to the lambardar. He retied his turban, then greeted the officer loudly, 'Salaam, Sardar Sahib.'

The officer looked away.

Imam Baksh started again. 'Everything is all right, isn't it, Sardar Sahib?'

The officer turned around abruptly and snapped, 'Get along. Don't you see I am busy?'

Imam Baksh, still adjusting his turban, meekly joined the villagers.

When both the trucks were loaded, the officer told Banta Singh to come to the camp next morning for the money. The trucks rumbled off toward the station.

Banta Singh was surrounded by eager villagers. He felt that he was somehow responsible for the insult to Imam Baksh. The villagers were impatient with him.

'O Lambardara, why don't you tell us something? What is all this big secret you are carrying about? You seem to think you have become someone very important and don't need to talk to us any more,' said Meet Singh angrily.

'No, Bhai, no. If I knew, why would I not tell you? You talk like children. How can I argue with soldiers and policemen? they told me nothing. And didn't you see how that pig's penis spoke to Chacha? One's self-respect is on one's own hands. Why should I have myself insulted by having my turban taken off?'

Imam Baksh acknowledged the gesture gracefully. 'Lambardar is right. If somebody barks when you speak to him, it is best to keep quiet. Let us all go to our homes. You can see what they are doing from the tops of your roofs.'

The villagers dispersed to their rooftops. From there the trucks could be seen at the camp near the station. They started off again and went east along the railway track till they were beyond the signal. Then they turned sharp left and bumped across the rails. They turned left again, came back along the line toward the station and disappeared behind the train.

All afternoon, the villagers stood on their roofs shouting to each other, asking whether anyone had seen anything. In their excitement they had forgotten to prepare the mid-day meal. Mothers fed their children on stale leftovers from the day before. They did not have time to light their hearths. The men did not give fodder to their cattle nor remember to milk them as evening drew near. When the sun was already under the arches of the bridge everyone became conscious of having overlooked the daily chores. It would be dark soon and the children would clamour for food, but still the women watched, their eyes glued to the station. The cows and buffaloes lowed in the barns, but still the men stayed on the roofs looking toward the station. Everyone expected something to happen.

The sun sank behind the bridge, lighting the white clouds which had appeared in the sky with hues of russet, copper and orange. The shades of grey blended with the glow as evening gave way to twilight and twilight sank into darkness. The station became a black wall. Wearily, the men and women went down to their courtyards, beckoning the others to do the same. They did not want to be alone in missing anything.

The northern horizon, which had turned a bluish grey, showed orange again. The orange turned into copper and then into a luminous russet. Red tongues of flame leaped into the black sky. A soft breeze began to blow towards the village. It brought the smell of burning kerosene, then of wood. And then—a faint acrid smell of searing flesh.

The village was stilled in a deathly silence. No one asked anyone else what the odour was. They all knew. They had

115

known it all the time. The answer was implicit in the fact that the train had come from Pakistan.

That evening, for the first time in the memory of Mano Majra, Imam Baksh's sonorous cry did not rise to the heavens to proclaim the glory of God.

The Woman on Platform 8

Ruskin Bond

IT WAS MY SECOND YEAR AT boarding-school, and I was sitting on platform no. 8 at Ambala station, waiting for the north bound train. I think I was about twelve at the time. My parents considered me old enough to travel alone, and I had arrived by bus at Ambala early in the evening: now there was a wait till midnight before my train arrived. Most of the time I had been pacing up and down the platform, browsing at the bookstall, or feeding broken biscuits to stray dogs; trains came and went, and the platform would be quiet for a while and then, when a train arrived, it would be an inferno of heaving, shouting, agitated human bodies. As the carriage doors opened, a tide of people would sweep down upon the nervous little ticket-collector at the gate; and every time this happened I would be caught in the rush and swept outside the station. Now tired of this game and of ambling about the platform, I sat down on my suitcase and gazed dismally across the railway-tracks.

Trolleys rolled past me, and I was conscious of the cries of the various vendors—the men who sold curds and lemon, the sweetmeat-seller, the newspaper boy—but I had lost interest in all that went on along the busy platform, and continued to stare across the railway-tracks, feeling bored and a little lonely.

'Are you all alone, my son?' asked a soft voice close behind me.

I looked up and saw a woman standing near me. She was leaning over, and I saw a pale face, and dark kind eyes. She wore no jewels, and was dressed very simply in a white sari.

'Yes, I am going to school,' I said, and stood up respectfully; she seemed poor, but there was a dignity about her that commanded respect.

'I have been watching you for some time,' she said. 'Didn't your parents come to see you off?'

'I don't live here,' I said. 'I had to change trains. Anyway, I can travel alone.'

'I am sure you can,' she said, and I liked her for saying that, and I also liked her for the simplicity of her dress, and for her deep, soft voice and the serenity of her face.

'Tell me, what is your name?' she asked.

'Arun,' I said.

'And how long do you have to wait for your train?'

'About an hour, I think. It comes at twelve o'clock.'

'Then come with me and have something to eat.'

I was going to refuse, out of shyness and suspicion, but she took me by the hand, and then I felt it would be silly to pull my hand away. She told a coolie to look after my suitcase, and then she led me away down the platform. Her hand was gentle, and she held mine neither too firmly nor too lightly. I looked up at her again. She was not young. And she was not old. She must have been over thirty but, had she been fifty, I think she would have looked much the same.

She took me into the station dining-room, ordered tea and samosas and jalebies, and at once I began to thaw and take a new interest in this kind woman. The strange encounter had little effect on my appetite. I was a hungry school boy, and I ate as much as I could in as polite a manner as possible. She took obvious pleasure in watching me eat, and I think it was the food that strengthened the bond between us and cemented our friendship, for under the influence of the tea and sweets I began to talk quite freely, and told her about my school, my friends, my likes and dislikes. She questioned me quietly from time to time, but preferred listening; she drew me out very well, and I had soon forgotten that we were strangers. But she did not ask me about my family or where I lived, and I did not ask her where she lived. I accepted her for what she had been to me—a quiet, kind and gentle woman who gave sweets to a lonely boy on a railway platform . . . .

After about half an hour we left the dining-room and began walking back along the platform. An engine was shunting up and down beside platform no. 8, and as it approached, a boy leapt off the platform and ran across the rails, taking a short cut to the next platform. He was at a safe distance from the engine, and there was no danger unless he had fallen; but as he leapt across the rails, the woman clutched my arm. Her fingers dug into my flesh, and I winced with pain. I caught her fingers and looked up at her, and I saw a spasm of pain and fear and sadness pass across her face. She watched the boy as he climbed the other platform, and it was not until he had disappeared in the crowd that she relaxed her hold on my arm. She smiled at me reassuringly, and took my hand again: but her fingers trembled against mine.

'He was all right,' I said, feeling that it was she who needed reassurance.

She smiled gratefully at me and pressed my hand. We walked together in silence until we reached the place where I had left my suitcase. One of my schoolfellows, Satish, a boy of about my age, had turned up with his mother.

'Hello, Arun!' he called. 'The train's coming in late, as usual. Did you know we have a new Headmaster this year?'

We shook hands, and then he turned to his mother and said: 'This is Arun, mother. He is one of my friends, and the best bowler in the class.'

'I am glad to know that,' said his mother, a large imposing woman who wore spectacles. She looked at the woman who led my hand and said: 'And I suppose you're Arun's mother?'

I opened my mouth to make some explanation, but before I could say anything the woman replied: 'Yes, I am Arun's mother.'

I was unable to speak a word. I looked quickly up at the woman, but she did not appear to be at all embarrassed, and was smiling at Satish's mother.

Satish's mother said: 'It's such a nuisance having to wait for the train right in the middle of the night. But one can't let the

119

child wait here alone. Anything can happen to a boy at a big station like this, there are so many suspicious characters hanging about. These days one has to be very careful of strangers.'

'Arun can travel alone though,' said the woman beside me, and somehow I felt grateful to her for saying that. I had already forgiven her for lying: and besides, I had taken an instinctive dislike to Satish's mother.

'Well, be very careful Arun,' said Satish's mother looking sternly at me through her spectacles. 'Be very careful when your mother is not with you. And never talk to strangers!'

I looked from Satish's mother to the woman who had given me tea and sweets, and then back at Satish's mother.

'I like strangers,' I said.

Satish's mother definitely staggered a little, as obviously she was not used to being contradicted by small boys. 'There you are, you see! If you don't watch over them all the time, they'll walk straight into trouble. Always listen to what your mother tells you,' she said, wagging a fat little finger at me. 'And never, never talk to strangers.'

I glared resentfully at her, and moved closer to the woman who had befriended me. Satish was standing behind his mother, grinning at me, and delighting in my clash with his mother. Apparently he was on my side.

The station bell clanged, and the people who had till now been squatting resignedly on the platform began bustling about.

'Here it comes,' shouted Satish, as the engine whistle shrieked and the front lights played over the rails.

The train moved slowly into the station, the engine hissing and sending out waves of steam. As it came to a stop, Satish jumped on the footboard of a lighted compartment and shouted, 'Come on, Arun, this one's empty!' and I picked up my suitcase and made a dash for the open door.

We placed ourselves at the open windows, and the two women stood outside on the platform, talking up to us. Satish's mother did most of the talking.

'Now don't jump on and off moving trains, as you did just now,' she said. 'And don't stick your heads out of the windows, and don't eat any rubbish on the way.' She allowed me to share the benefit of her advice, as she probably didn't think my 'mother' a very capable person. She handed Satish a bag of fruit, a cricket bat and a big box of chocolates, and told him to share the food with me. Then she stood back from the window to watch how my 'mother' behaved.

I was smarting under the patronizing tone of Satish's mother, who obviously thought mine a very poor family; and I did not intend giving the other woman away. I let her take my hand in hers, but I could think of nothing to say. I was conscious of Satish's mother staring at us with hard, beady eyes, and I found myself hating her with a firm, unreasoning hate. The guard walked up the platform, blowing his whistle for the train to leave. I looked straight into the eyes of the woman who held my hand, and she smiled in a gentle, understanding way. I leaned out of the window then, and put my lips to her cheek, and kissed her.

The carriage jolted forward, and she drew her hand away.

'Goodbye, mother!' said Satish, as the train began to move slowly out of the station. Satish and his mother waved to each other.

'Goodbye,' I said to the other woman, 'goodbye—mother . . . .

I didn't wave or shout, but sat still in front of the window, gazing at the woman on the platform. Satish's mother was talking to her, but she didn't appear to be listening; she was looking at me as the train took me away. She stood there on the busy platform, a pale sweet woman in white, and I watched her until she was lost in the milling crowd.

121

The Intimate Demon

Manoj Das

SHE WAS ASLEEP, MY LITTLE cherub, after a solemn understanding with me that a tiny real monkey must be procured for her as soon as possible, since she had for the first time in her life, ventured out to live without her mother. As I remembered the watchman of my bungalow rearing such a creature of a gentle, pacific breed, I happily consented to comply with her demand. The compensation she wanted for missing her mother for a week seemed reasonable.

The blue bulb that beamed anaemically dim in the solitude of my coupé and the moonlight that flowed in occasionally through the window, had gathered around my sleeping daughter the azure enchantment of the faery isles. I gazed at her and I gazed at the moon. I didn't have to dream as dreams seemed to have encircled me. I could retire to the upper berth, but did not, and relished the fear that she might fall down and it was necessary for me to keep sitting beside her.

The train was passing through mofussil stations, one after another, picking up passengers in ones and twos, breaking the gurgling din with interludes of rustic hullabaloo.

Thus had the hours of a midsummer's night a rhythmic

---

* There were no corridors or vestibules up to the 1960s. Each compartment was an independent unit. The trains had four classes: I, II, Inter and III.

passage until we reached what was only an apology for a
station with hardly a roof over its officer's head. The purpose
of a waiting-room was duly served by bushy trees all around
the tin-shed. But from this most unsuspected setting emerged a
big crowd which shook up the train as it jostled to board it in
the twinkle of an eye. There were blows against my door too.
But soon the train resumed movement and I could faintly see
the rump of the crowd, still sufficient for half a train, looking
blankly at the vanishing giant it had failed to tame.

Once more I carefully arranged the little pillow by my
daughter's side and prepared to climb to my upper berth. But
a turn of the train revealed a shadow by the window. As I
carefully observed through the glass, a big man, big even in his
beard, was discovered quietly hanging on. I was disgusted and
told myself that he deserved to be left where he was. But I
suspected that the fellow was dozing! If I had a slight misgiving
in regard to his character, it vanished. A thief could not afford
to doze.

I lifted the window glass and drew his attention. In harmony
with the jolly moon, a broad smile bloomed on his face. 'I am
a very humble man, sir,' he said. 'You are brave indeed, sir, to
hang on like that and manage a nap too,' I responded, opening
the door and waving him in.

He entered after some polite hesitation and sat down on the
floor. He informed me of some big festival, the cause of the
rush at the last station. People who had crossed the river to be
at the festival were obliged, on their return journey, to travel by
train up to the next station as the river had suddenly been in
spate and the ferry boat had got defunct.

'This is first class. I am sure, you have only a third class
ticket. But you can be here till your destination,' I said with a
touch of compassion.

The stranger introduced himself as a perpetual wanderer
with all his worldly belongings under his arm and assured me
that he had neither any ticket nor any destination.

I gave up the idea of going to sleep. But the monotony of
the chugging train lulled me for a while.

A shrill sound stabbed my repose. I sat bolt upright and
tried to locate the source of the noise. My daughter was still

asleep. It was the old man. He had started playing a flute.

What he did was by no means diabolical. But, I do not know why, I was seized by a fury. He appeared to me the very symbol of fiendishness and ingratitude. Even though I knew that I should not mind the sound, the thought that the sleep I had secured for my daughter after hours of effort meant so little to the intruder made me burst out, 'Stop!'

He looked at me rather bewildered and, without a word, put the flute back in his worn-out haversack and stood up with some effort. The train had stopped at another station. He opened the door and, silently saluting me, got down.

As I closed the door and turned back, I was unhappy to see my daughter awake, in the process of sitting up. I switched on the main light.

'Why did you get up, my child?' I murmured. She remained silent for a moment and then, grabbing me as I sat down by her side, said softly, 'I was dreaming such a beautiful dream, Papa!'

'Good. What was it about?'

She was already in tears. 'I was wandering in a charming garden, full of flowers and fairies. Among them was a wonderful child. He played his flute to me. But then, you know . . . .'

Her voice choked. I wiped tears off her cheeks. 'But then, what happened?' I asked.

She recovered and continued, 'Suddenly someone thundered at him and rushed upon him. It was a big, bad demon. His music stopped. All around there were clouds. I do not know what happened after.'

I looked through the window. The sleeping meadows were flooded with moonlight. But I was waking up to darkness and a demon lurking—somewhere inside.

A Stranded Railroad Car

Intizar Husain

'ALL OF THIS, BROTHER, MEANS nothing. To tell you the truth, travel isn't enjoyable any more.'

Bundu Miyan's story was heard with great interest. But Shujat Ali somehow didn't care for this concluding remark and said, 'Well now, I wouldn't go that far. Travel must have meant quite a lot to our elders. Why else would they have stirred out of doors? They weren't crazies. You are too young and inexperienced to jump to conclusions. All you had was a single trip, which ended somewhat badly for you. And right away you decide there's no fun and adventure in travel. As I look at it, you never took a journey—I mean a real travel, which is something else again. Well, Mirza Sahib, what do you think?'

Mirza Sahib gently removed the spout of the hookah from his lips, opened his drowsy eyes, cleared his throat, and said, 'Shujat Ali, you shouldn't argue with these modern boys. What do these *kids* know about travelling! Especially the train—it's taken all enjoyment out of journeying. You blink your eye and you've arrived at your destination. But there was a time when kingdoms fell and governments toppled by the time you reached where you were going, and the toddlers you'd left crawling naked on all fours—you returned to find them fathers worrying their heads over a suitable match for their marriageable daughters.'

The idea of political upheavals caught Bundu Miyan's fancy.

He couldn't resist remarking, 'Mirza Sahib, even entire governments topple down today in less time than it takes to blink an eye. You go to the booking counter, purchase your ticket, hop on the train, and at the very next stop you can already hear, the hawker yelling about a coup somewhere.'

'Oh, yes, just a coup. Nothing more and nothing less,' Mirza Sahib was quick to remark. 'But in the past,' he continued, 'a change of government invariably meant a change of coinage too. New monarch, new coins. That was a real journey, one hell of a journey. One went on travelling hundreds and hundreds of miles, back and forth, with the destination nowhere in sight and all traces of a starting point irretrievably obscured. Each journey seemed to be the last. Just imagine the hazards attending a journey in the past: the fear of tigers, of snake-bites, of highwaymen and, yes, of ghosts too. You had neither clocks nor electricity in those days. You travelled by the dim, starlit sky overhead and the burning torches below. A torch suddenly blown out by the wind and your heart dropped between your feet; a meteor shot in the sky leaving behind a blazing trail, and your heart pounded fitfully, and you prayed, 'Lord God! take care of us and don't let us wayfarers down!' And now—the night's spent before you know it. Back then, though, it took ages to pass a single night in travel; a night then meant the span of a century.'

Mirza Sahib was left speechless. So were Bundu Miyan and Manzur Husain. The mouthpiece of the hookah froze between Shujat Ali's lips; only the pipe's gurgle, rising in an incessant monotone, fell gently upon the darkening portico where it blended with the tranquil silence of nightfall.

Mirza Sahib resumed his chatter in a manner that seemed to suggest he had strayed too far and was now back to the point. 'No horse-drawn carts, no journey. Today the train is in fashion. I just don't feel like travelling any more. By God, only one journey is left now. But come to think of it, who needs a carriage for that one? Off I shall go when my time's come . . .' he sighed and lapsed into silence.

The spout was still stuck as before under Shujat Ali's grey moustache, and the gurgling went on as a matter of course. Then Sharfu, the servant, emerged from the house, holding a

lantern. The darkening portico lit up dimly and there was a
slight stir. Sharfu pulled up a stool near the chairs, set the
lantern upon it, and raised the wick a little. Shujat Ali gently
passed the spout to Mirza Sahib, who tried a puff or two, then
quickly let go of it, peering at the chillum—the clay bowl atop
the hookah. It's gone cold,' he murmured. Then raising his
voice he called the servant, 'Sharfu! Put some fresh tobacco in.
A few burning coals too.'

Shujat Ali pushed his chair back for no apparent reason. He
yawned languidly, passed his palms over his wrinkled cheeks,
and spoke in a measured tone, 'You could not be more right,
Mirza Sahib. Travelling really has changed a lot these days. But
. . . but a journey, after all, is a journey, whether you travel by
horse-cart or by train.'

'But even in a train journey . . . ' Mirza Sahib wanted to say
something, God knows what, but Shujat Ali grabbed the thread
instead and went on, 'Yes, even in a train journey you witness the
most bizarre things and encounter strange sorts of people . . . .'

'. . . and you get to see a face or two which, in its infinite
charm, becomes etched on your heart forever; it stays with you
and you are never quite able to forget it,' said Manzur Husain,
suddenly remembering a long-forgotten incident. And with
this, he felt the overwhelming urge to narrate it. And why not,
if Bundu Miyan could tell such a long yarn. The incident had
occurred an eternity ago, and yet how was it, Manzur Husain
wondered, that he hadn't told a soul about it? Suppose he told
them—what could he possibly lose? At his age who would
suspect him of anything unseemly or foul?

Manzur Husain was about to speak when Bundu Miyan
burst out, 'Look at him. He fancies meeting charming faces.
God, I never could believe there are people who travel looking
just for romances!'

'Miyan, you've got it all wrong,' Shujat Ali interrupted. 'A
train is a whole city in miniature. Hundreds of people get in or
get off at every stop. You are bound to rub shoulders with all
sorts of people in the crowd.'

'If you rub shoulders, inevitably you may meet the eyes too.
Listen, I would like to tell you something,' Manzur Husain was at
it at last. Bundu Miyan's offensive attitude had warmed him up.

But it was Shujat Ali who cut him short this time. 'Eyes meeting eyes—what's so unusual about that? You could be at home and still exchange glances with the girl in the balcony across the street. Why set out on a journey when you could accomplish as much right here at home? Well, stunning things happen while travelling. At times, the very history of a country takes on a new turn.' Shujat Ali had warmed up now. 'Well, Mirza Sahib,' he said, 'you would scarcely remember the time when the railway first came here. We were mere kids then, weren't we? My late father used to tell us about it.'

Manzur Husain waited for Shujat Ali to finish recounting his tale so that he might begin his. But the latter seemed bent on spinning a fresh and longer yarn. In time Manzur Husain's restiveness began to lessen of its own accord. He persuaded himself in different ways: that it ill-behoved a middle-aged man like himself to cackle about such matters, that he doesn't seem to remember the whole story anyway, that some links were missing, that it was like an incoherent dream, neither fully remembered, nor totally forgotten. The dream appeared very hazy to begin with, except for a single bright spot which by the minute grew brighter still. It was a tawny face—full of charm. The spot of light began to expand and illuminated a foggy corner of his memory: a bunch of weary passengers who sat half-awake, half-asleep inside a dimly-lit waiting-room. He was himself ensconced in a chair, drowsing. Then he dozed off, but the clatter of wheels outside woke him up. The train was late, yet he somehow felt it had steamed in. He darted out to make sure, and found a freight train chugging along. He remained on the platform a while, pacing up and down, and then returned to the waiting-room, where from time to time he furtively glanced at the bench opposite him. It was occupied by a heavy, squat man with salt-and-pepper hair clad in a white dhoti and a long coat that came all the way to his knees, and a slim young woman of a delightfully tawny complexion huddled beside him. She too was drowsing. Whenever her onion-coloured sari slipped off her head, her long, luxuriant, jet-black hair flashed in the light and a pair of delicate, pale earrings, dangling from her lobes, emitted sparks . . . .

Shujat Ali was narrating his story with gusto: 'Both Hindus

and Muslims kicked up quite a fuss. They said their holy saints were buried here, so no railroad tracks were going to be laid here. But the British were in no mood for such pious insanities. Why would they be? They were the rulers. And they were drunk with power. The railroad track was laid down anyway. It was then that my father was obliged to take a trip to Delhi,' Shujat Ali paused for a moment. In a tone swelling with pride, he continued, 'My father was the first in this city to ride the train. Even the big shots hadn't seen a train until then—why, a lot of them hadn't even heard of it . . . . '

Manzur Husain was not listening to the words, but only to the voice of the narrator; staring hard at him, desperately hoping for him to stop at some point. Gradually the narrator's face grew hazy and his voice dimmed. The bright spot became exceedingly luminous . . . those illuminated corners and crannies, flashing bright lines . . . . It was a long railroad track along one side of which ran an interminable line of lampposts quietly shedding the gentle glow of their light bulbs. The bright cone of light around a lamppost, the darkness beyond it, the black iron tracks vanishing into the distance. He had unrolled his bed on an upper berth; on the lower berths some passengers were comfortably stretched out and sleeping; others were uncomfortably stuffed in narrow spaces and simply drowsing, their heads resting against windows. From time to time somebody would wake up, turn over on his side, glance casually at the sleeping passengers, and doze off again. Many stations passed by; many times the train slowed down and came to a halt. The dark car suddenly lit up, followed by a din as the passengers jostled to climb aboard or jump down and peddlers barged in to sell their wares. The whistle, the jerk, and once again the incessant clatter of wheels. As the train picked up speed, the same familiar feeling assaulted him: as if the car he was riding in had come unhitched and stood stranded in the middle of nowhere while the rest of the train, whistling and clattering, had steamed far away. Sometimes he felt as if the train had started running backwards, pulling time along with it, and that the night would never end. Half the span of a century had passed and the other half was yet to pass; that the train wasn't really going forward—it was merely moving in circles, spinning as it were, on a pivot; that when it stopped it seemed it would remain standing all night long, and when it moved, it seemed like it would go on racing with the night, competing with it but never quite outwitting it. And then the train would slow down again, as if its wheels had become too tired to turn any more; the same flood of light in the dark car; the din of motley passengers, porters, peddlers; people suddenly waking from their sleep and inquiring, 'Is this a junction?'—a semi-articulate expression sinking into the depths of sleep. 'No, it's only some small station'; whistles, more whistles; the familiar jerk; the same heavy clatter of lazy wheels. He looked at his watch. 'Only one-thirty!' he was surprised. Many times he had dozed off and many times been awakened; still the night seemed to have barely waned—on the contrary, it seemed to have become even longer. He got up wearily, climbed down from his berth and made for the toilet. On the lower berth, the squat man in the white, flowing dhoti and long coat had dozed off, and was now snoring away heavily. The young woman beside him with the delightful tawny complexion, with sleep strung in her eyes, her head propped up against the window, looked inebriated. A sudden gust of wind blew her dark, lustrous curls and scattered them all over her face. The edge of her sari too had slipped off her chest, revealing the contours of a pair of beautifully firm, round breasts. The sheer beauty of her blossoming youth enthralled him for a moment or two. It was absolutely quiet inside the compartment; the passengers were asleep, and the only sound came from the incessant clatter of wheels. It was so hot inside that the man sitting in the opposite corner had removed even his undershirt. Suddenly he got up and blurted out, 'The black river's just ahead.' With an ever-increasing clatter of wheels the train entered a tunnel. He stood where he was as the train emerged from one darkness and plunged into another. It grew pitch dark inside the car . . his thoughts abruptly derailed.

'No sooner had the train reached the bank of the River Jamuna than it ground to a halt, smack in the middle of the jungle,' Shujat Ali was continuing with his narrative. 'Midnight! What to do? The times were especially bad. Highwaymen roamed about freely throughout the country. Even in Delhi one dared not go past the banks of the Jamuna without putting one's life in grave danger. Well, anyway, they thoroughly checked the engine but found nothing wrong with it. Still, it just wouldn't budge. An endless night, the jungle with its myriad sounds, each more frightening than the next, and no habitation near or far in which to look for shelter—it was some experience. The night came to an end eventually. At the crack of dawn, in the first, hesitant light, people saw a saintly looking grey-bearded man quietly saying his prayers huddled in the corner of one of the cars. Having said his prayers, the hoary old man looked at the people and said, 'Have the railroad track dug up!'

Bundu Miyan found himself gawking at Shujat Ali. Mirza Sahib, wishing to draw on the hookah, felt unable to raise the spout to his mouth. His hand froze, and his grip around the pipe tightened. Manzur Husain, however, was busy retrieving the missing links in his memory.

After a pause Shujat Ali looked up at Mirza Sahib and resumed, 'People went and reported this bizarre incident to the British officer. He flew into a rage. But there was little he could do. The train simply wouldn't budge. He relented. He agreed to have the track dug out—his hands were tied. A whole slew of labourers was called in and the digging got underway. They had barely dug down a few feet when they discovered an underground vault . . . . ' Shujat Ali broke his narrative to look awhile at Mirza Sahib, Bundu Miyan and Manzur Husain, who all sat perfectly motionless, like images cast in stone. He resumed: 'My father used to tell us how three armed men, mustering all their courage and repeating the name of the Lord, descended into the vault. And what did they see but a magnificent hall. A brand new clay pot of fresh water—filled, as if only moments ago—standing in a corner, its top covered by an upturned silver bowl. Nearby on the floor an aged, saintly figure in white clothes, with a lily-white beard and eyebrows, sat on a mat quietly telling his beads . . . . '

Shujat Ali's voice seemed to be receding. Manzur Husain's mind was changing tracks again. A string of irregularly illumined dots whirred round and round before him. The illumined dots magnified themselves into bright, scintillating

131

images of remarkable clarity . . . . The train rushed through the tunnel with piercing noise and reckless speed. The dark water below rose up in gentle waves to kiss the tracks. His lips quivered, his fingers throbbed with sweet warmth. The young woman's disquietingly lovely face, her warm fleshy body—that bright and sparkling image left a ray in his eyes—a ray which penetrated many dark corners and flooded them with light. Early next morning when he got down from his berth his eyes met with hers for a mere second and then travelled through the window to the comfort of the cool and refreshing dawn outside. Their eyes met one more time, when she and the man in the white dhoti got down to change trains. The other train stood along the platform nearby. Clouds of smoke billowed out from the locomotive, dissipated in the fresh morning air and eventually dissolved. There was a whistle. The stationary wheels hissed a little and then got into motion. The locomotive sent up curls of black smoke. Immediately, there was another whistle, and his train too began to pull out. The two trains ran parallel a little way, then the distance between them widened and they drifted apart, gathering speed. Her train moved farther and faster away. The cars in her train, jammed with passengers, moved past him like images in a movie. Finally, even that car went past him in which her face, despite its tawny complexion, somehow appeared the sharpest, the brightest. Her train merged into the distant woods; only the baggage car trailing behind it remained visible for a while longer; then it too vanished into the lush, green space beyond . . . .

'When they looked a second time, there was absolutely nobody on the mat.' That was Shujat Ali still narrating his story.

'And the saintly figure—where did he go?' Bundu Miyan asked with surprise.

'God knows,' Shujat Ali replied. 'Only the clay pot still stood in its place, but it was empty.'

'You mean the water too had vanished?' Bundu Miyan's surprise knew no bounds.

'Yes, it had.' Shujat Ali's voice was now a mere whisper. 'My father used to say that the Sepoy Revolt broke out the very next year; the Jamuna turned into a river of fire, and Delhi was razed to the ground.'

Shujat Ali became silent. Mirza Sahib, too, sat in wordless immobility. Bundu Miyan went on gazing at Shujat Ali. Manzur Husain yawned wearily and pulled the hookah towards himself. A minute later he said, poking into the *chillum,* 'It's cold again.'

Mirza Sahib sighed deeply, 'Nobody knows the mysteries of God.' He then yelled, 'Sharfu, put some tobacco in!'

The dim corners and crevices had now assumed a soft, bright translucence, allowing those random images to coalesce into a coherent scene, perfectly intact, lacking in none of its details. Manzur Husain felt excited. The long-forgotten incident had returned to him as vibrant as reality. He was dying to recount it, the whole of it, to the others, withholding nothing, with brio and magnificence. He repeatedly looked at Mirza Sahib, Bundu Miyan and Shujat Ali, impatiently waiting for the spell created by Shujat Ali to wear off, so that he could get on with his own tale. When the hookah was brought back, he drew a few puffs and passed it on to Shujat Ali, saying, 'Have a few puffs—it is fresh now.' Shujat Ali took the pipe and started to smoke.

Manzur Husain began impatiently, 'Something happened to me too—something truly bizarre.'

An indifferent Shujat Ali kept himself busy smoking, but Bundu Miyan evinced a genuine interest, 'Oh, what?'

Mirza Sahib's expression gave nothing away; all the same, his eyes had become riveted to Manzur Husain's face.

Manzur Husain was suddenly feeling very tense; at the end of his wits. He didn't know quite where and how to begin. Shujat Ali pushed the hookah away and started to cough. Manzur Husain grabbed the hookah with nervous alacrity and drew impatiently on it a few times.

'Well?' Bundu Miyan urged.

'It happened when I was very young. Now it all seems so very odd.' Manzur Husain fell into thought again.

By now Shujat Ali, too, had become fully attentive. Manzur Husain took a few more puffs on the hookah and coughed for no reason at all. 'It happened that . . . ' he faltered. He was about to start again when, unexpectedly, the sight of a number of flickering lanterns, followed by the rising, dull sound of light footfalls, came from the alley up ahead. Manzur Husain looked at the approaching lanterns inquisitively and then asked, 'Mirza Sahib, who could that . . . ?' He could not finish his sentence.

In the meantime Sharfu, feeling alarmed, had come out of the house. Mirza Sahib instructed him, 'Go find out and let us know!'

Sharfu was soon back, panting, 'Nothing in our lane,' he informed. 'These are men from the hucksters' lane . . . the son of Shammas the huckster . . . .'

'The son of Shammas the huckster?' Bundu Miyan was visibly shaken. 'But I myself saw him minding his shop this morning—he was quite all right then.'

'Yes, yes. He was quite all right until this afternoon,' said Sharfu. 'He had his lunch, then felt some pain in his chest. By the time the doctor arrived . . . .'

'Good Heavens!' exclaimed Mirza Sahib. 'This cardiac arrest is almost a racket these days. Never heard of the sickness while we were young. Isn't that right, Shujat Ali?'

Shujat Ali heaved a deep sigh and nodded absentmindedly. Mirza Sahib too drifted off into his own thoughts. Bundu Miyan and Manzur Husain were also silent. Sharfu remained standing, hoping that they would start talking again and allow him the opportunity to provide some more information. But, after a while, feeling disappointed, he decided to go back inside. Then, abruptly, he turned, raised the wick in the flickering lantern and poked at the chillum in the hope of somehow stirring the silent men. They could not be moved. So Sharfu went inside.

After a long pause Shujat Ali broke the silence, sighing, 'Well, that's the way of the world. People are born and people die. There's no escaping the inevitable. Manzur Husain, you were going to tell us something—weren't you?'

'Sure you were,' Bundu Miyan chimed in, returning from his silence.

Manzur Husain shuddered, pulled himself up to speak, but soon drifted off into his thoughts again. 'The whole thing is gone off my mind,' he mumbled. Those luminescent spots in his mind had again plunged into darkness. The railroad car had come unhitched and stood alone in the tracks, stranded in the middle of nowhere, while the rest of the train had steamed away—far, far away.

'What a pity!' Mirza Sahib exclaimed, promptly falling back into his reverie.

Shujat Ali pulled the hookah towards himself. He drew on the spout a few times, coughed, then began puffing with some regularity.

Manzur Husain's mind had gone completely blank. He was still struggling to dredge out of it whatever he could when his son suddenly appeared and announced, 'Abbaji, dinner is ready.'

Manzur Husain took it as a godsend. He got up, climbed down the few steps of the portico, and hurried off to his home. It had begun to get dark in the alley. The lamppost at the corner had been lit, quietly shedding a cone of light, beyond which was darkness. A blind beggar finding his way in the darkness with his staff, the sound of dim footfalls coming from a casual pedestrian, a door slamming shut somewhere . . . . By the time Manzur Husain reached home the dim spots had assumed a renewed brilliance, and the same oppressive urge to tell his story was nagging at him once again—to rescue that dazzling ray from the darkness and expose it in all its glory to the world. He abruptly turned around and said, 'Son, you go in. I'll be along soon.' He was going back to Mirza Sahib's portico.

The street had become darker still in the meantime. The neighbourhood children, who had raised such a racket until a little while ago, had all gone home. Only a couple of daredevils still remained. They stood near the bathroom of the mosque where a firelight had been burning in a small niche in the wall. They had scraped enough soot to roll into a few black marbles to play with. The fuel had burned out; merely smouldering embers remained. The soot on the wall was getting harder to scrape. Manzur Husain went past the mosque, entered the side lane, and made for Mirza Sahib's. He found the chairs on the portico empty, but the hookah and the lantern were still there.

'Where is Mirza Sahib, Sharfu?'

'At the mosque—to perform his evening prayer; he'll be back any minute. Do sit down, please.'

Manzur Husain flopped down, back in his old chair. He sat

there for quite a long while and drew a few times on the hookah but it had gone cold.

'Shall I get some fresh fire and tobacco?' Sharfu asked.

'No, never mind. I think I will go home.'

Manzur Husain got up and went home the way he had come.

Barin Bhowmik's Ailment

Satyajit Ray

Mʀ Bᴀʀɪɴ Bʜᴏᴡᴍɪᴋ ɢᴏᴛ ɪɴᴛᴏ compartment D as instructed by the conductor and placed his suitcase under his seat. He would not need to open it during his journey. But he must keep the other smaller bag somewhere within easy reach. It contained such essentials as a comb, a hair brush, a toothbrush, his shaving kit, a book by James Hadley Chase to read on the way and several other knick-knacks, including throat pills. If the long train journey in a cold, air-conditioned compartment resulted in a sore throat, he would not be able to sing tomorrow. He quickly popped a pill into his mouth and put his bag on the small table before the window.

It was a Delhi-bound vestibule train. There were only about seven minutes left before its departure, and yet there was no sign of the other passengers. Would he be able to travel all the way to Delhi all alone? Could he indeed be so lucky? That would really be the height of luxury. The very idea brought a song to his lips.

He looked out of the window at the crowd on the platform. Two young men were glancing at him occasionally. Clearly, he had been recognized. This was not a new experience. People often recognized him for many were now familiar not just with his voice but also with his appearance. He had to give live performances at least half a dozen times every month. Listen to Barin Bhowmik tonight—he will sing songs written by Nazrul as well as *aadhunik*. Money and fame—both had come to Barin Bhowmik in full measure.

However, this had happened only over the last five years. Before that he had had to struggle a lot. It was not enough to be a talented singer. He needed a suitable break and proper backing. This came in 1963 when Bhola-da—Bhola Banerjee—invited him to sing in the Puja pandal in Unish Palli. Barin Bhowmik had not looked back since then.

In fact, he was now going to Delhi at the invitation of the Bengal Association to sing at their jubilee celebrations. They were paying for his travel by first class and had promised to make all arrangements for his stay in Delhi. He intended spending a couple of days in Delhi. Then he would go to Agra and Fatehpur Sikri and return to Calcutta a week later. After that it would be time for Puja again and life would become madly hectic.

'Your order for lunch, sir . . . ?'

The conductor-guard appeared in the doorway.

'What is available?'

'You are a non-vegetarian, aren't you? You could choose between Indian and Western food. If you want Indian, we've got . . . .'

Barin placed his order for lunch and had just lit a Three Castles cigarette when another passenger came into his compartment; the same instant, the train began pulling out of the station.

Barin looked at the newcomer. Didn't he seem vaguely familiar? Barin tried to smile, but his smile vanished quickly as there was no response from the other. Had he made a mistake? Oh, God—how embarrassing! Why did he have to smile like an idiot? A similar thing had happened to him once before. He had thumped a man very hard on the back with a boisterous, 'Hel-lo, Tridib-da! How *are* you?' only to discover he was not Tridib-da at all. The memory of this incident had caused him much discomfort for days afterward. God laid such a lot of traps to embarrass one!

Barin Bhowmik looked at the other man once more. He had kicked off his sandals and was sitting with his legs outstretched, leafing through the pages of the latest *Illustrated Weekly*. Again,

Barin got the feeling that he had seen him somewhere, and not just for a few minutes. He had spent a long time in this man's company. But when was it? And where? The man had bushy eyebrows, a thin moustache, shiny hair and a little mole in the middle of his forehead. Yes, this face was certainly familiar. Could he have seen this man when he used to work for Central Telegraph? But surely the whole thing could not have been one-sided? His companion was definitely not showing any sign of recognition.

'Your order for lunch, sir?'

The conductor-guard had reappeared. He was a portly, rather amiable, gentleman.

'Well,' said the newcomer, 'we'll worry about lunch later. Could I have a cup of tea first?'

'Of course.'

'All I need is a cup and the beverage. I prefer drinking black tea.'

That did it. Barin Bhowmik suddenly began to feel rather unwell. There was a sinking feeling in the pit of his stomach. Then it seemed as though his heart had grown wings and flown straight into his lungs. It was not just the man's voice but also the words he uttered with a special emphasis: black tea. That was enough to remove the uncertainties from Barin's mind. Every memory came flooding back.

Barin had indeed seen this man before and that too— strangely enough—in a similar air-conditioned compartment of a train going to Delhi. He himself was going to Patna to attend the wedding of his cousin, Shipra. Three days before he left, he had won a little more than seven thousand rupees at the races. He could, therefore, afford the luxury of travelling by first class. This happened nine years ago, in 1964, long before he had become a well-known singer. He could vaguely recall the other man's surname. It began with a 'C'. Chowdhury? Chakravarty? Chatterjee?

The conductor-guard left. Barin realized he could no longer sit facing the other man. He went and stood in the corridor outside, well away from his fellow passenger. Yes, coincidences did occur in life. But this one was unbelievable.

But had 'C' recognized him? If he had not, there might be

two reasons for it. Perhaps he had a weak memory. Or perhaps Barin's appearance had undergone significant changes in these nine years. He stared out of the window and tried to recall what these changes might possibly be.

He had gained a lot of weight, so presumably his face now looked fuller than it had before. He did not wear glasses in those days. Now he did. And his moustaches had gone. When did he shave them off? Ah yes. Not very long ago. He had gone to a salon on Hajra Road. The barber was both young and inexperienced. He failed to get the symmetry right while trimming the moustaches. Barin himself did not notice it at first; but when everyone in his office from the chatty old liftman, Sukdeo, to the sixty-two-year-old cashier, Keshav Babu, began commenting on it, he shaved his precious moustaches off totally. This had happened about four years ago.

So he had lost the moustaches, but gained a bit of flesh on his cheeks and acquired a pair of glasses. Feeling a little reassured, he returned to his carriage.

A bearer came in with a pot of tea and placed it in front of C. Barin, too, felt the need for a drink, but did not dare speak to the bearer. What if C recognized his voice?

Barin did not want even to think about what C might do to him if he did get recognized. But, of course, everything depended on the kind of man C was. If he was anything like Animesh-da, Barin had nothing to fear. Once, in a bus, Animesh-da realized someone was trying to pick his pocket. But he was too shy to raise a hue-and-cry, so he practically gave away his wallet to the pickpocket, together with four crisp ten-rupee notes. He told his family afterwards, 'A big scene in a crowded bus with me playing a prominent role in it—no, I could not allow that to happen.'

Was this man a bit like that? Probably not. People like Animesh-da were hard to come by. Besides, his looks were not very reassuring. Everything about him—those bushy eyebrows, the blunt nose and that chin that jutted out—seemed to suggest that he would not hesitate at all to plant his hairy hands on Barin's throat and say, 'Are you not the same man who stole my clock in 1964? Scoundrel! I have spent these nine years looking for you! Today, I shall . . . .

140

Barin dared not think any more. Even in this air-conditioned compartment there were beads of perspiration on his forehead. He stretched himself out on his berth and covered his eyes with his left arm. It was one's eyes that gave one away. In fact, C had seemed familiar only because Barin recognized the look in his eyes.

He could now recall every incident vividly. It was not just the matter of stealing C's clock. He could remember every little thing he had stolen in his life ever since his boyhood. Some were totally insignificant things like a ballpoint pen (Mukul Mama's), or a cheap magnifying glass (his classmate, Akshay's), or a pair of bone cuff-links that belonged to Chheni-da and which Barin did not need at all. He never wore them even once. The only reason he stole these—and, for that matter, all those other things—was that they were near at hand and they belonged to someone else.

Between the ages of twelve and twenty-five, Barin Bhowmik had removed at least fifty different things from various people and made a collection in his house. What could one call it but stealing? The only difference between him and a regular thief was that a thief stole to survive in life; Barin did it out of habit. Nobody ever suspected him. He had, therefore, never been caught. Barin knew that this habit, this strange compulsion to steal things, was a kind of illness. Once he had even learnt the medical term for it from one of his friends who was a doctor, but now he could not remember what it was.

But C's clock was the last thing he had stolen. In the last nine years, he had never experienced that sudden, strong urge. He knew he had got over his illness and was now totally cured.

The difference between stealing C's clock and all the other petty thefts he had indulged in was that he had really wanted that clock. It was a beautiful travelling clock, made in Switzerland. It lay in a blue square box and stood upright the moment the lid was lifted. It was an alarm clock and the sound of the alarm was so sweet that it was a pleasure to wake up to it.

Barin had used that clock consistently over these nine years. He took it with him wherever he went. Even today, the clock was resting within the depths of the bag kept on the table before the window.

141

'How far are you going?'

Barin gave a violent start. The other man was actually speaking to him!

'Delhi.'

'Pardon?'

'Delhi.'

The first time, in an effort to disguise his voice, Barin had spoken so softly that the man had clearly not heard him.

'Do you find it a bit too cold in here? Is that what's affecting your voice?'

'N-n-no.'

'It can happen, of course. Actually, I would have preferred going by ordinary first class if it wasn't for the dust.'

Barin did not utter a word. He did not want to look at C, but his own curiosity forced him to cast frequent glances in C's direction. Was C showing signs of recognition? No. He appeared quite relaxed. Could he be pretending? But there was no way of being sure. After all, Barin did not know him well. All he had learnt the last time about his fellow passenger was that he liked having black tea and that he was wont to get down at every station to buy snacks. Thanks to this habit, Barin had had the chance to eat a lot of tasty stuff.

Apart from this, Barin had seen one other side to C's character, just as they were about to reach Patna. This was directly related to the incident involving the clock.

They had been travelling by the Amritsar Mail. It was supposed to reach Patna at 5 a.m. The conductor came and woke Barin at 4.30. C, too, was half awake, although he was going up to Delhi.

Just about three minutes before the train was to reach Patna, it suddenly screeched to a halt. What could be the reason? There were a few people with torches running about on the tracks. Was it anything serious? In the end, the guard turned up and said that an old man had been run over by the engine while crossing the track. The trail would start as soon as his body was removed.

C got very excited at this news and clambered down quickly in the dark, still clad in his sleeping suit. Then he went out to see for himself what had happened.

It was during this brief absence that Barin had removed the clock from C's bag. He had seen C wind it the night before, and had felt tempted immediately. But since the chances of finding a suitable opportunity were dim, he had told himself to forget the whole thing. But, when an opportunity presented itself so unexpectedly, Barin simply could not stop himself. Even at the risk of being seen by the other passenger lying on the upper berth, he had slipped his hand into C's bag and had taken the clock out. Then he had dropped it into his own case. It took him between fifteen and twenty seconds to do this. C had returned about five minutes later.

'A horrible business! A beggar, you see. The head's been totally severed from the body. I fail to see how an engine can possibly hit somebody despite a cow-catcher. Isn't it supposed to push aside all obstacles on the track?'

Barin got off safely at Patna and was met by his uncle. The faint uneasiness in the pit of his stomach vanished the instant he got into his uncle's car and, drove off. His heart told him that that was the end of the story. No one could catch him now. The chances of running into C were one in a million; or perhaps even less than that.

But who knew that one day, years later, by such an incredible coincidence, they would meet again? 'A thing like this is enough to make one turn superstitious,' Thought Barin to himself.

'Do you live in Delhi? Or Calcutta?' asked C.

He had asked him a lot of questions the last time as well, Barin recalled. He hated people who tried to act friendly.

'Calcutta,' said Barin. Oh no! He had spoken in his normal voice. He really must be more careful.

Good God—why was the man staring so hard at him? What could be the reason for such interest? Barin's pulse began beating faster again.

'Did your photograph come out in the papers recently?'

Barin realized it would be foolish not to tell the truth. There were other Bengali passengers on the train who might recognize him. There was no harm in telling this man who he was. In fact, if he could be told that Barin was a famous singer, he might find it difficult to relate him to the thief who had once stolen his clock.

143

Satyajit Ray

'Where did you see this photograph?' Barin threw a counter question.

'Do you sing?' came another one.

'Yes, a little.'

'Your name . . . ?'

'Barindranath Bhowmik.'

'Ah, I see. Barin Bhowmik. That's why you seemed familiar. You sing on the radio, don't you?'

'Yes.'

'My wife is an admirer of yours. Are you going to Delhi to sing at some function?'

'Yes.'

Barin was not going to tell him much. If a simple 'yes' or 'no' could suffice, there was no need to say anything else.

'I know a Bhowmik in Delhi. He's in the Finance Ministry. Nitish Bhowmik. Is he a relative or something?'

Indeed. Nitish was Barin's first cousin. A man well known for his rigid discipline. A close relative, but not one close to Barin personally.

'No, I'm afraid I don't know him.'

Barin decided to tell this one lie. He wished the man would stop talking. Why did he want to know so many things?

Oh good. Lunch had arrived. Hopefully, the volley of questions would cease, at least for a little while.

And so it did. C was obviously one who enjoyed eating. He began to concentrate on his food and fell silent. Barin no longer felt all that nervous, but still he could not relax completely. They would have to spend at least another twenty hours in each other's company. Memory was such a strange phenomenon. Who could tell what little thing—a gesture, a look, a word— might make some old and forgotten memory come to life?

Black tea, for instance. Barin believed that if those two words had not been uttered, he would never have recognized C. What if something he said or something he did made C recognize *him*?

The best thing, of course, would be not to say or do anything at all. Barin lay down on his berth, hiding his face behind his paperback. When he finished the first chapter, he turned his head cautiously and stole a glance at C. He seemed

144

to be asleep. The *Illustrated Weekly* had dropped from his hand onto the floor. An arm was flung across his eyes, but from the way his chest rose and fell it seemed as though he had fallen into a deep sleep. Barin looked out of the window. Open fields, trees, little huts—the barren landscape of Bihar flashed past. The noise of the wheels came very faintly through the double glass of the windows, sounding as though, in the far distance, a number of drums were being beaten in the same steady rhythm: *dha-dhinak, na-dhinak, dha-dhinak, na-dhinak* . . . .

Another sound from within was soon added to this: the sound of C's snoring.

Barin felt a lot more reassured. He began humming a Nazrul song. His voice did not sound too bad. He cleared his throat once and began to sing a bit more loudly. But he had to stop almost immediately.

Something else was making a noise in the compartment. It shocked Barin into silence.

It was the sound of an alarm clock. The alarm on the Swiss clock kept in his bag had somehow been set off. And it continued to ring, non-stop.

Barin discovered he could not move his limbs. They were paralyzed with fear. His eyes fixed themselves on C.

C moved his arm. Barin stiffened.

C was now awake. He removed his arm from his eyes.

'Is it that glass? Could you please remove it? It's vibrating against the wall.'

The noise stopped the instant Barin took the glass out of the iron ring attached to the wall. Before placing it on the table, he drank the water that was in it. This helped his throat, but he was still in no mood to start singing again.

Tea was served a little before they reached Hazaribagh Road. Two cups of hot tea and the absence of any further curious questions from C helped him relax more. He looked out once again and began humming softly. Soon, he was able to forget totally the danger he was in.

At Gaya, not unexpectedly, C got down on the platform and returned with two packets of peanuts. He gave one of them to Barin. Barin consumed the whole packet with considerable relish.

The sun had set by the time they left the station. C switched the lights on and said, 'Are we running late? What's the time on your watch?'

Barin realized for the first time that C was not wearing a watch. This surprised him and he could into help but show it. Then he remembered that C's question had not been answered. He glanced at his wristwatch. 'It's 7.35,' he said.

'Then we're running more or less on time.'

'Yes.'

'My watch broke this morning. It was an HMT . . . gave excellent time . . . but this morning someone pulled my bedsheet so hard that the watch fell on the ground and . . . . '

Barin did not comment. Any mention of watches and clocks was reprehensible.

'What make is your watch?' asked C.

'HMT.'

'Does it keep good time?'

'Yes.'

'Actually, I have always been unlucky in the matter of clocks.'

Barin tried to yawn, simply to assume an unconcerned air, but failed in his attempt. Even the muscles in his jaw appeared to be paralyzed. He could not open his mouth. But his ears continued to function. He was forced to hear all that C had to say.

'I once had a Swiss travelling clock, you see. Made of gold. A friend of mine had brought it from Geneva. I had used it for barely a month and was carrying it with me on a train to Delhi—exactly like this, you know, in an air-conditioned compartment like this. There were only two of us—another Bengali chap. Do you know what he did? Just think of his daring! In my absence—while I may have gone to the bathroom or something—he nicked that clock from me! He looked such a complete gentleman. But I suppose I'm lucky he didn't murder me in my sleep. I stopped travelling by train after that. This time, too, I would have gone by air, but the pilots' strike upset my plans . . . . '

Barin Bhowmik's throat was dry, his hands felt numb. But he knew if he said absolutely nothing after a tale like that, it

146

would seem odd. In fact, it would seem distinctly suspicious. With a tremendous effort, he forced himself to speak.

'Did . . . did you not look for it?'

'Ha! Can any stolen object be found simply by looking for it? But, for a long time, I could not forget what the man looked like. Even now I have a vague recollection. He was neither fair nor dark, had a moustache and must have been about the same height as you, but was slimmer. If I could meet him again, I would teach him a lesson he'd remember all his life. I was a boxer once, you know. A light heavyweight champion. That man is lucky our paths never crossed again . . . . '

Barin could now remember the full name of his companion. Chakravarty. Pulak Chakravarty. Strange! The minute he mentioned boxing, his name flashed in Barin's mind like a title on a television screen. Pulak Chakravarty had talked a lot about boxing the last time.

But even if his name had come back to him, what good did it do? After all, it was Barin who was the culprit. And now it had become impossible to carry his load of guilt. What if he went and confessed everything? And then returned the clock? There it was in that bag . . . so near at hand . . . !

No! Was he going mad? How could he entertain such thoughts? He was a famous vocalist. How could he admit to having stooped so low? Would his reputation not suffer? Would anyone ever invite him to sing at their function? What would his fans think? Where was the guarantee that this other man was not a journalist or someone connected with the media? No, there was no question of making a confession.

Perhaps there was no need for it, either. Perhaps he would be recognized, anyway. Pulak Chakravarty was giving him rather odd looks. Delhi was still sixteen hours away. There was every chance of being caught. In Barin's mind flashed a sudden image—his moustaches had grown back, the flesh on his face had worn away, his glasses had vanished. Pulak Chakravarty was staring hard at the face he had seen nine years ago. The look of amazement in his slightly hazel eyes was slowly turning into a look filled with anger. His lips were parting in a slow, cruel smile. 'Ah ha!' he seemed to be saying, 'you *are* the same man, are you not? Good. I have waited all

147

these years to lay my hands on you. Now I shall have my little revenge . . . .'

By 10 p.m., Barin had acquired a fairly high temperature, accompanied by intense shivering. He called the guard and asked for an extra blanket. Then he covered himself from head to foot with both blankets and lay flat on his back. Pulak Chakravarty closed the door of their compartment and bolted it. Before switching off the lights, he turned towards Barin and said, 'You appear unwell. I have some very effective pills with me—here, take these two. You're not used to travelling in an air-conditioned coach, are you?'

Barin swallowed the tablets. Well, given his present condition, Chakravarty might spare him a ruthless punishment. But Barin had made up his mind about one thing. He must transfer that clock to the suitcase of its rightful owner. He must try to get this done tonight, if possible. But he could not move until his temperature went down. His body was still shivering occasionally.

Pulak had switched on the reading lamp over his head. He had a paperback open in his hand. But was he reading it, or was he only staring at a page and thinking of something else? Why did he not turn the page? How long could it take to read a couple of pages?

Suddenly Barin noticed Pulak's eyes were no longer fixed on the book. He had turned his head slightly and was looking at Barin. Barin closed his eyes. After a long time, he opened one of them cautiously and glanced at Chakravarty. Yes, he was still staring hard at Barin. Barin promptly shut his eyes again. His heart was jumping like a frog, matching the rhythm of the wheels—*lub dup, lub dup, lub dup.*

A faint click told him that the reading light had been switched off. Slightly reassured, he opened both his eyes this time. The light in the corridor outside was coming in through a crack in the door. Barin saw Pulak Chakravarty put his book down on the table beside Barin's bag. Then he pulled his blanket up to his chin, turned on his side, facing Barin, and yawned noisily.

Barin's heartbeats gradually returned to normal. Tomorrow— yes, tomorrow morning he must return the clock. He had noticed Pulak's suitcase was unlocked. He had gone and changed into a sleeping suit only a little while ago.

Barin had stopped shivering. Perhaps those tablets had started to work. What *were* they? He had swallowed them simply so that he would recover in time to be able to sing at that function in Delhi. Applause from an audience was something he had no wish to miss. But had he done a wise thing? What if those pills . . . ?

No, he must not think about such things. The incident of the glass vibrating against the wall was bad enough. Obviously, all these strange ideas were simply a result of a sick and guilt-ridden mind. Tomorrow, he must find a remedy for this. Without a clear conscience, he could not have a clear voice and his performance would be a total failure. Bengal Association . . . .

The tinkle of tea cups woke Barin in the morning. A waiter had come in with his breakfast: bread, butter, an omelette and tea. Should he be eating all this? Did he still have a slight fever? No, he did not. In fact, he felt just fine. What wonderful tablets those were! He began to feel quite grateful towards Pulak Chakravarty.

But where was he? In the bathroom, perhaps. Or was he in the corridor? Barin went out to take a look as soon as the waiter had gone. There was no one in the corridor outside. How long ago had Pulak left? Should he take a chance?

Barin took a chance, but did not quite succeed in his effort. He had taken the clock out of his own bag and had just bent down to pull out Pulak's suitcase from under his berth, when his fellow passenger walked in with a towel and a shaving kit in his hands. Barin's right hand closed around the clock. He straightened himself.

'How are you? All right?'

'Yes, thank you. Er . . . can you recognize this?'

Barin opened his palm. The clock lay on it. A strange determination had risen in Barin's mind. He had got over the old compulsive urge to steal a long time ago. But this business of playing hide-and-seek, was this not a form of deception? All that tension, those uncertainties, the anxiety over should-I-do-it-or-shouldn't-I, this funny, empty feeling in his stomach, the parched throat, the jumping heart—all these were signs of a malady, were they not? This, too, had to be overcome. There could never be any peace of mind otherwise.

Pulak Chakravarty had only just started to rub his ears with his towel. The sight of the clock turned him into a statue. His hand holding the towel remained stuck to his ear.

Barin said, 'Yes, I am that same man. I've put on a bit of weight, shaved my moustaches and have started wearing glasses. I was then going to Patna and you to Delhi. In 1964. Remember that man who got run over by our train? And you went out to investigate? Well, I took your clock in your absence.'

Pulak's eyes were now looking straight into Barin's. Barin saw him frowning deeply, the whites of his eyes had become rather prominent, his lips had parted as though he wanted to say something but could not find speech.

Barin continued, 'Actually, it was an illness I used to suffer from. I mean, I am not really a thief. There is a medical term for it which escapes me for the moment. Anyway, I am cured now and am quite normal. I used your clock all these years and was taking it with me to Delhi. Since I happened to meet you— it's really a miracle, isn't it?—I thought I'd return it to you. I hope you will not hold any . . . er . . . against me.'

Pulak Chakravarty could do no more than say 'thanks' very faintly. He was still staring at the clock, now transferred to his own hand, totally dumbfounded.

Barin collected his toothbrush, toothpaste, and shaving kit. Then he took the towel off its rack and went into the bathroom. He broke into song as soon as he had closed the door, and was pleased to note that the old, natural melody in his voice was fully restored.

* * *

It took him about three minutes to get N.C. Bhowmik in the Finance Ministry in Delhi. Then, a deep, familiar voice boomed into his ear.

'Hello.'

'Nitish-da? This is Barin.'

'Oh, so you've arrived, have you? I'm coming this evening to hear you sing. Even *you* have turned into a celebrity, haven't you? My, my, who would have thought it possible? But anyway, what made you ring me?'

'Well—do you happen to know someone called Pulak Chakravarty? He is supposed to have been your batch-mate in college. He knew boxing.'

'Who? Old Pincho?'

'Pincho?'

'Yes, he used to pinch practically everything he saw. Fountain pens, books from the library, tennis racquets from our common room. It was he who stole my first Ronson. It was funny, because it wasn't as though he lacked anything in life. His father was a rich man. It was actually a kind of ailment.'

'Ailment?'

'Yes, haven't you ever heard of it? It's called kleptomania. K-l-e-p . . . .'

Barin put the receiver down and stared at his open suitcase. He had only just checked into his hotel and started to unpack. No, there was no mistake. A few items were certainly missing from it. A whole carton of Three Castles cigarettes, a pair of Japanese binoculars and a wallet containing five hundred-rupee notes.

Kleptomania. Barin had forgotten the word. Now it would stay etched in his mind—forever.

Balbir Arora Goes Metric

 *Bill Aitken*

INDIA'S METRE GAUGE POSSESSES A magic of its own. Not only is it more leisurely than the broad gauge imposed by Lord Dalhousie but it gives you more of the essential India, being the only line that can claim to be pan-subcontinental. It runs from Fazilka in the cotton-picking tracts of Punjab all the way south to Tiruchendur in Tamil Nadu where a famous therapeutic temple stands on the ocean shore. In the east it runs from Ledo in Assam, whence 'Vinegar Joe's' Stilwell Road took off over the bamboo hump into Indo-China, all the way to Bhuj and in the desert province of Kutch and beyond to the Arabian Sea. The beauty of the metre gauge to the aesthetic traveller is that it remains rural in its concerns and leans to the curve of natural contours. It does not blast out broad Euclidian proofs that the shortest distance between two points is expensively direct but rather insinuates itself to the lie of the land, traversing up-river in Bihar to choose the least offensive bridging point or veering serpentwise in Madhya Pradesh to outwit the Vindhyan demand for tunnels.

Above all, the metre gauge is free of the population explosion that swamps its bigger budgetary rival. Move from Old Delhi's seething BG platforms with their high, inelegant insulation of tin and asbestos sheets and you come to the scaled down beauty of the metre bays with fine wrought-iron work surviving from a superior age on display when quality of workmanship seemed more important than the strident splash of posters with their litany of mass demands. Life along the metre gauge is unfrazzled and bookings for a second class sleeper coach can usually be done the same day you travel. The ease of spacious metric journeying provides a welcome respite from the scrum of main-line jostlings.

To the student of railway lore and lover of the iron horse the metre gauge also gives the bonus of steam traction and, fortuitously for the aesthete, the most resilient stable of *YP* express locos, (matched by their goods variant the *YG*) which are scaled-down models of the handsome 'Niagaras' that epitomized the golden age of American steam trains in their classic coupling of performance and style, speed and reliability. Though battered and now kept running only by the innovative ingenuity of Indian railwaymen long after their intended life-span, these big-hearted steam engines will see out the prescribed span for coal-fired motive power. Probably no other locomotive in India gives as much pleasure as these ancient blinkered Telcos (built by Tata at Jamshedpur thirty years ago), especially if you catch them at work on a branch line. The declining fleet of broad gauge *WP's* with their sleek bullet-nosed boilers might appear more flashy but even flat out at speed (a measly 45 mph) they seem dwarfed by the width of double track and score less on the scale of 'steam at work' which requires both frantic visibility of working parts and the urgent poetics of sibilant pistons. The difference between diesel and steam is the hiatus between a tossed back best-seller and the lingering savour on the palate that betokens true literature. Whereas we toast the best-selling author's cleverness but dump his work amongst the empties, so the modest impact of being pulled by diesel is instantly forgettable. Contrast the deep musical rumbling echoes of Dr Johnson or Sir Thomas Browne in the stately flow of liveried words. How very apt that with the decline and fall of the steam age these metre gauge veterans should conjure from their leaking glands the sonorous tread of Edmund Gibbon.

If I have been carried away by the orchestral performance of a working *YG* on a branch line, toiling round tight curves deep into the lush jungles of North Kannada with screaming flanges outsirened by the *whee-whee-wheeee* of her blind whistle as she carves a course through the nodding bamboo fronds that brush the driver's face as he strains to read his signal, it is only fair to give the other side of the metre gauge reckoning. Let us cease from the backwoods ballad of unremunerative traffic, (where I am the sole ticket-holding passenger on the empty 211 Up Alanavar-Dandeli Mixed) and switch to the upmarket symphony of the money-spinning 'Palace on Wheels', (POW) whose music is every bit as fascinating.

When I received an invitation from the Press Information Officer at Rail Bhavan—the assiduously spruced and polished headquarters of Indian Railways whose corridors are immaculately free of that depressing symbol of unmet official targets, the spittoon—my first instinct was to decline the offer to ride a brand new rake that heralded a modernized version of the dollar-raking 'Palace on Wheels'. For a start the freelance writer has only his credibility to fall back upon and once the public associates his outpourings with the subsidized slant of sponsors he is effectively vasectomised. By accepting a free ride at Indian Railways' expense would I not be announcing my thraldom to official policy and fall into the silken trap of preferring to flatter my hosts rather than stigmatize my reputation with the label of *namak harami*? It was for such times of moral dilemma and intellectual indecision that God presumably created women. 'don't be an idiot,' said Prithwi, my companion of twenty years. 'Think of all the debts written off and your time and energy wasted by government servants, plus the fact that you have always gone out of your way to give Indian Railways a good write-up. They owe you this trip.' It was true that I had invested a lot of time and expense in tracking down aspects of Indian railway history that appealed to me but no one expects a refund for real pleasures enjoyed. Sadly, however, time and again my researches were hindered by the very railwaymen I had set out to magnify. Even when armed with letters of permission from the highest level in Delhi to visit loco sheds and other similar vintage assets where the security risk was absolutely minimal I found spite and harassment awaiting my researches and access to historically valuable evidence stymied by the dog in the manger attitudes of pettyminded railwaymen. It took years for it to dawn why this rash urge of regional railwaymen to cross swords with Delhi should be provoked by my harmless presence. Then one day I saw some metre gauge sidings being whitewashed and a flurry of flunkeys descend to announce the arrival of the special coach of their chief engineer on a tour of inspection. By the time he came, all the scams that his arrival should have checked had been conveniently swept under the carpet. Indian Railways as one of the world's biggest employer's maintains a staff of such huge proportions that there is bound to be scope for hanky panky in alienating public property into the hands of private parties. The untimely arrival of persons like myself in such situations could only trigger off panic followed by the bluff that the dictates of Delhi did not run here.

The same flurry of flunkeys greeted my arrival at Delhi cantonment where the inaugural run of the new luxury rake would be flagged off by the Rail *mantri*. I confess my opinion of the POW had been pretty low mainly from its disappointing reputation for actual railway atmosphere. It was more a snob's tour of Rajasthan's palaces, according to friends who had paid its steepish fare. Confirmed rail travellers who had been on the Venice Simplon Orient, the Trans Siberian and South Africa's Blue Train all complained that from the railway angle they had felt short-changed by the old POW. Also they had found the original saloons of the Rajputana maharajas hot, dusty and grinding and it was for this reason, we were told, Indian Railways had decided to build a new, air-conditioned rake to seek to capture the mood of princely travel but in greater comfort.

The reception arrangements were chaotic and had it not been for the two superbly caparisoned YG steamers (sent down the line from Bandikui) simmering in all their buffed splendour, I might have turned on my heel and declined to put my fate in the hands of such incompetents. After furious consultations of lists, everyone of which seemed to differ, I was shown to a smart, three-bedded cabin. One's first impressions of the train would have been marvellous had it not been for the flapping officials racing up and down trying to match their incompatible lists. Exhausted even before the train had got up steam, I

155

scooped up the bed-side trinkets bearing the Palace logo (soap, pen and notepaper) as souvenirs. Hardly had I stowed away my perks when the officials announced I must move. It appears that because my name sounded American I had been awarded a cabin to myself. But on discovering that I was a mere Indian they asked me to kindly move down to the back of the train and share a cabin with a fellow journalist.

When I related the story to Subhash Kirpekar, the parliamentary reporter of the *Times of India*, he immediately worked out a solution to avoid any further demotions from the prestigious rank of Yank. I should insist my initials 'B.A.' refer to an irrefutable Indian identity. Thus for the duration of the week on wheels I would answer to the appellation 'Balbir Arora'.

The initial reaction of the press to their luxurious cabins was relief that they did not have to pay, especially in view of the somewhat cramped quarters. There was also criticism of the poor watering of passengers, and passing along the sleek carpeted corridors of the ivory-exteriored coaches one could hear several groans as over-optimistic latherers found the water pressure inadequate to dislodge their soap suds. At a press conference in Jaipur the railway authorities admitted to a few 'teething problems' but had no answer to the charge that real maharajas would not have bathed from plastic buckets. But with the unpredictability of the water supply the status of buckets had become academic. The critics shook the dust of the Palace off their wheels and returned to Delhi to describe our new train as a cruel hoax. Significantly none of the European tourists on board complained. Perhaps the problem lay in the broad gauge perceptions of the critics. Not many countries exceed the British standard gauge so that your average tourist does not expect to flourish his elbows on a train. Press critics from the Gangetic tracts accustomed to plenty of water and pampered with stretching space failed to adjust to the metric restraints of the desert. Another distracting feature for the main line passenger is that his trajectory through the night, thanks to the BG coupling, follows the flight of the arrow whereas the single-link of the metre gauge coach emulates the yaw of a yacht. Add to this the fact that the fast lines are continually upgraded with ballast onto which secure cement sleepers are laid and you have a much smoother ride. Also, the big trunk routes now have welded rails that delete the clickety-clicks of the old ninety pounder lines though to the railway buff this breakthrough is hardly viewed as a virtue. Not only has the music fled but the speed of the train for the cerebrally minded is now less easily calculated. What is a railway after all without its clicks and clacks?

The tourist attractions of the POW make it a bargain package and no one has ever complained that Rajasthan Tourism fell short on its promises to reveal a dizzying round of princely residences. In fact the only criticism I heard was that the Railways, partner in the POW venture went overboard and exposed the leg-weary tourists to so many palaces that Rajasthan's royal lifestyle began to come out of their ears. I was no stranger to Rajasthan's fecundity in the matter of feudal fastnesses and took good care on this repeat visit to curtail my explorations to only the very best of the palatial pickings. That meant sitting out Jaipur and Jodhpur and waiting for Udaipur and Jaisalmer to arrive. Even then one could not escape converted forts and palaces doubling as restaurants when it came to eat. While the stationary buffet lunches at these five star establishments were satisfactory and for the most part laid out amidst splendidly impressive (not quite the same as saying 'useless') settings, the tastiest food undoubtedly was served on the train's two dining cars. Here again a metre gauge diner is hardly the place for two all-in wrestlers to sit cheek by jowl but in view of the presence of several slim lady journalists the seating arrangements were always satisfactorily resolved. One of the tour's most lasting impressions was the contrast between the graceful femininity of the Indian Press contingent and the hefty input of overseas unshapeliness. (Great beefy memsahibs who found the 'outsize' in Indian ready-made garments shops too small were politely referred to try the 'Russian' size.)

There is an obvious price to be paid for all this feudal *fol-de-rol* and it comes out in the arrogance of the palace staff towards tourists—to be followed by an instant flip to servility of the most gross order when one of the erstwhile royal families appears. Unlike lesser seats where this schizophrenic switch from growling bulldog to grovelling pi has been made into a fine art, Udaipur gives you the true impress of royalty with its subtly understated graces. Like the sun from which the rulers of this elegant state are descended, they have nothing to prove and Udaipur's atmosphere in every way is a cut above Jaipur's rather gross display of pomp. But in one feature Jaipur scores over its senior rival. The view over the city at night from yet another palace on the hilltop (shown to me by Teki Tejwal, the *Statesman* photographer) was unforgettable.

Jodhpur's main fort of Mehrangarh is another dominating experience but the wonderful architectural integrity of the city has been seriously compromised by the modern Ummaid Bhavan palace, a modern triumphal ode to mindless opulence. Built as a drought-relief project, one can only suggest that during the next drought the dismantling of this vulgar eyesore would bring relief to the outraged skyline. Jaisalmer is in a class of its own and must rank as one of the world's most improbable fairytale towns. Its architecture is fused to the desert landscape and the artistry of its citizens amidst such hostile elements makes the mess of India's bigger cities, where people take no pride in their easier surroundings, all the more culpable.

Another delightful halt took place in Chittoragarh but we were so pressed for time that it might have been kinder to have left it out, not from any shortcoming of the ruins but simply because its superior mix of architecture and history demands proper respect. The line of Udaipur cuts through some rugged scenery and ahead the marble quarries of the Aravallis lead up to the great ghat section from Kamblighat to Phulad. The princely quality of these ex-royal lines can still be seen in the stone-work of the stations. Unfortunately our tight schedule at Udaipur caused the POW to run late and miss the right of way on to the tight curves of the descent. That meant going down at dusk and depriving this railway buff the mechanical highlight of the week's run. Special engines were once shedded at Kamblighat to ease the trains down but today YPs do the job gingerly. Our train all the way from Bandikui (which we had reached in the middle of our first night out of Delhi) had been hauled by a YDM4 diesel and the driver had no qualms at taking her down the tortuous ghat line with his twenty-one coaches. In fact he welcomed a TV crew aboard to film the descent. (At last I had come across one advantage that diesel locos have over steam—standing room in the cab.)

As Kamblighat is a recognized watering hole for thirsty steamers I thought this would be the time to have a bath in the tricky shower on wheels. For once the pressure was right but owing to the buck and slew of the train as it screamed round the sharp unwinding ghat I found the water going everywhere except where it was intended. I made a note of the fact that in the hugely restricted bathroom the waste-pipe of the W.C. stuck out from the wall a full ten inches. As every inch counted one wondered how the Russian size of passenger fared in his ablutions.

Sleeping in the train was most comfortable and here the only complaint (from my Kerala cabin-mate) was that the air-conditioning was too fierce. Several less actively disposed passengers also queried the intensive tourist routine and would have preferred to relax more on board rather than traipse around palace basements with their oddball collections of princely paraphernalia that ranged from collapsible commodes to Prussian spiked helmets. The disappointment of the steam fan was aggravated by promises of steam engines that never appeared. Such official attempts at soothing indignant reactions were fatal especially when the aggrieved party seemed to be more realistic about railway working than the expert paid to lecture him. If coal-fired locos could not be found on the main line how would they be fuelled at Jaisalmer in the middle of the desert? Most annoying of all was to hear the final promise that steam would be made available for the final stretch back into Delhi. Thus for the first time on the whole trip the photographer could capture the POW hauled by a steam engine in the full light of day. But when we did reach Delhi, by the time Balbir Arora from the rear of the long train had rushed down to get his long-awaited bonus, both engines had decoupled and were seen as disappearing specks down the line. They had decamped for watering, having posed for the full satisfaction of the Yankee cameramen housed in the front portion of the train.

Companionship between press and tourists overcame all the minor irritants and everyone's chief fear in view of the

159

outstanding and varied menus on board was that they would be too bulky to get down again from the dining car. The bar was something of a joke, done up in black gleaming plastic-laminate with silvered designs that made the most sober instinctively reach for a drink. (It was more like Las Vegas than Rajasthan.) But it also doubled as a lounge and overcame a very serious running defect of our inaugural train. The distinctively named carriages had their corridor connections sealed off on the grounds that this would encourage privacy and a family feeling amongst the confined passengers. But in practice one suspected it was caused by the basic metric bug-bear of lack of space. At the end of each coach was housed a chief bearer with his butling assistant, both donned in the traditional attire of their province. They had to cook and housekeep and act as security guards against hordes of curious bystanders, as well as appear unflapping at all times before their sahibs. The cribbed arrangements meant that their pantry shelves by day were turned into bunks at night, though in fact one of ours thought it more comfortable to sleep on the floor of the small dining lounge at the other end of the coach, where we had breakfast or watched video films. It was the temptation of the latter that caused the butler to turn himself into a guard at night.

One thoughtful input of the train designers (the whole rake was conceived and constructed at the Perambur Coach Factory in an incredible six months) was to leave the windows of our individual lounges open so that the true railway lover could stick his head out in the time-honoured custom of his tribe. If there is one monstrous shortcoming of air-conditioning it is in the cocooning of passengers away from the passing scene. Sometimes as one sat looking out of the elegant oval window that was set in our lounge door one could see a passenger train pull up alongside with rustic travellers clinging to the roof, desperate evidence of poverty and horrendous inequality. As a minor saving grace from the charge of privileged right of way, the POW enjoyed no VIP status and had to give precedence to the daily scheduled stock.

The most serious grumble came from the railway crew themselves, especially the men manning the air-conditioning coach. They found it difficult to buttonhole a journalist who would write about their grievance rather than review the exterior gloss of their smartly painted rake. Apparently in the rush to get the Palace on the road the logistics of housing and feeding the support staff had not been worked out. Now they found they had to eat off station platforms and sleep at their work places. To get drinking water at a wayside station in Rajasthan is not the easiest of tasks, as I found out when I got up early to see the desert sun climb crimsonly over the golden ramparts of Jaisalmer. I asked a local camel driver where they got their water and he pointed to the ground. A well had to go down 300 feet before the crucial layer was struck. But after the sweat of drilling, the reward was to find sweet and *mazboot pani* (as the locals described it).

That day in Jaisalmer began disappointingly. As usual when the train got in late we could expect garlands. The critical hour was 10 a.m. because before that the local tourist officer legally need not bestir himself. A cynic in the party thought that all our reception parties looked alike. Were they, their drums, tilaks and garlands, stuffed after the ceremony in the brake-van to follow us for the next off loading? The buses arranged by Rajasthan Tourism to take us from the station to the prescribed unwheeled palaces included a local guide who on the whole performed well. The best was a young man in Udaipur whose commentary matched the class of the city's palaces. The worst was undoubtedly the layabout who thoroughly demoralized our party's opinion of Jaisalmer. His main job appeared to be that of commission agent for he was much more concerned to linger at handicraft shops than display the town's remarkably rich architectural heritage. Incredibly, this nincompoop persuaded the whole party to avoid looking over the fort palace on the flimsy grounds that it was 'empty'. In point of fact the emptiness of Jaisalmer's magical fortification is a thousand times more fulfilling than trudging past the grandiose clutter of Rajasthan's other regal basements.

At the Jaisalmer railway station we had pulled up in our blue-lined ivory livery alongside a genuine royal saloon. The local Maharaja hires out his saloon to parties who prefer the real thing, in spite of the heat and dust these old mahogany bodied coaches are heir to. At Jaipur, in the sidings, the observant visitor could spot the original POW rake awaiting a decision on its redeployment. Apparently one pressing reason for substituting the old carriages by new was not for the cosmetic need to meet modern standards of appearance (replacing real leather bar stools piped with brass studs with rexine coverings fixed with tin tacks) but to satisfy safety standards. A whole rake of highly inflammable coaches is hardly an incentive to railway officers to work out ways to speed up its schedule.

There was talk that a second metre gauge Palace would be introduced in the south to accommodate the vintage but now idle rake. Called 'Heritage on Wheels' it would run on a circuit of Karnataka and Goa lines taking in the cornucopia of India's southern cultural delights, including Shravanbelgola, Belur, Halebid, Aihole, Badami and Hampi plus the beaches of Goa beyond the ghat line from Londa. The danger here might be to repeat the excess of Rajasthan's too rich diet. Probably a little more of railway interest and less emphasis on tourist sites would result in more pleasant recollections of Karnataka's sensational cultural circuit. The forests along the line make for magnificent viewing and the riotous greenery of the Sahyadris is a tourist delight in itself.

Everyone on the train was by now complaining of indigestion both cultural and culinary. Big meals followed the endless tramp round fusty forts and the menu was so seductive that commonsense invariably lost out to satiation. The oldies in the group began to wilt from the pace and were forced to choose between a swim in the five star pool of our lunch rendezvous or shop for local handicrafts. As the sole steam specialist I boarded a local passenger parked alongside our train and went down the line to the Udaipur loco shed to try and find any predecessor to the *YP*. Jaipur had yielded a *YL* but so reluctantly that its loco shed foreman seemed to think I had just landed from Mars.

Cameras, like alcohol, are forbidden fruits on Indian railways. However read the rules carefully for the more morally doubtful of the two and you discover that consumption of the latter is only proscribed (in best feudal tradition) for the lower orders.

Injustice seems bitterly compounded when those already cramped in plebeian circumstances are expected to abstain (though there is nothing in the rules that expressly forbids a second-class passenger from sticking his head out of the window and having a swig when his train passes through a tunnel.)

Such dilemmas did not assault our itinerary and ensconced amidst the luxury lounge's Rajasthani decor (which extended to a silk painted ceiling, one sipped the local tonic that came more profitably from the stationary *deshi tekka* than our moving glitzy bar. *Kesar kasturi* is the desert equivalent of 'Highland cream' and its soporific fall-out after a sensuous mouthful of flame recalls the old Hebridean motto: 'There's no such thing as a bad whisky: they all make you immortal.' There is logic and magic in comparing the distilled spirit with the mysteries of steam traction. Just as water boiled by simple chemistry expands to rejuvenate the dance of molecules, so the spirit of the railway traveller soars with his metric tot of saffron and musk.

The final stage of our by now thoroughly enjoyable ride through the desert brought us to the scruffy but homely station of Agra Fort. Metre gauge stations unlike their renovated (read 'destroyed') counterparts on the broad gauge still command a lot of affection from the student of steam's golden days. On the overnight journey back to Delhi by the *chhoti* line (the BG gets you there in four hours) are several delightfully preserved platforms where the station-master's office still houses an ancient clock and bulky furniture from an age that preceded the coming of the Pickford removal van. Bandikui junction is a delightful period piece, not just a station but a whole railway town laid out in open country, similar to Swindon when Brunei designed his rail workers cottages. The pecking order in Bandikui is sternly apparent from the size of the bungalow you are allotted. But sprawling bougainvillaea has tended to even out the apartheid of hierarchy. A magnificent church spire soars forlornly in search of a congregation from the midst of what was once its hallowed yard but is now a blaze of golden wheat.

But first the Taj Mahal summoned our attentions. Thanks to the rigorous security precautions we were made to enter by the police quarters so that our initial vision of the tear-drop on the cheek of eternity was through the drying underpants on a police washing line. Lunch was held in another Taj and as conviviality flowed on this penultimate celebration the management decided to drop a hint that, as far as they were concerned, the party was over. (Their subtle signal was to switch off all the lights.) But our group was not to be dislodged so easily. When it was whispered to the food and beverage manager that the climax to our tour had been ruined and that our company had been just about to surprise one of its members with a rendering of 'Happy birthday to you' the mellow mood was re-established. As I joined in the chorus, slightly miffed that my birthday had passed—the chairman of the tourist corporation had offered to stand the lucky person a drink in the POW bar that night—I heard the winner's name, oddly familiar . . . 'Happy birthday dear Balbir Arora, happy birthday to you.'

Railway Reverie

R.K. Laxman

SHEKAR ENTERED THE TRAIN compartment and made his way along, bumping against people and assorted baggage left in the narrow corridor. When he finally found his seat he almost collapsed into it.

The whole day had been spent running around tying up things left to the last minute. He collected his laundry from the U.N. Laundry & Drycleaners, packed his suitcase, gathered the books and papers scattered all over his room and stuffed them haphazardly on the shelf, went hunting for the sweeper to clean up the room, stood in an endless, near immobile queue at the bank to encash a cheque, went to the post office to put through a long-distance call to his mother to inform her about the time of his arrival but abandoned the effort after several attempts. Then he went to his landlady to hand over the key to his paying guest room to which he had moved sometime ago and told her he would be back in a fortnight. When he had finished all this he had just enough time to pick up his luggage and rush to the railway station.

He looked around to gauge the advantages of the berth he occupied and was satisfied with his window seat but felt that the fan was not angled to benefit him much.

There were too many people crowding the compartment. Shekar hoped that most of them would get off before the train started. Some were already saying goodbye. There were a few engaged in giving or receiving last minute instructions, advice. There were others who were just hanging on looking bored and glancing at their watches every few minutes. Shekar thought he could write an article 'Impressions Gathered in a Railway Compartment'. Of course, he would add a lot more details to make it hilarious reading. As he was pondering over this theme he felt someone tapping his elbow. He turned round and saw the coolie who had brought his luggage. He stood there scratching his head, waiting for Shekar to pay him off. Shekar had completely forgotten his presence. He apologized and taking out his purse, gave him some money. The coolie was all set to grumble and make his habitual demand for extra payment when he saw the denomination of the currency note on his palm and slunk away hurriedly.

'Too much, too much! You are spoiling the greedy fellows ...' came a voice from a corner.

'Do you know how much these chaps earn per day?' continued the voice. Shekar took some time to locate it in the crowd. It belonged to a fat chap. He smiled and said, 'That's all right. It does not hurt me to pay a little more to these coolies occasionally. I don't travel very often, you see . . . . '

'But we do. These fellows expect the same extravagant payment from us also . . . . '

Shekar was in no mood to carry on the argument. But the fat fellow continued, 'Do you know how much I used to pay these coolies ten years ago?' Some passengers came in between them at this point and obstructed the view. The fat man leaned sideways and shouted, 'You know how much? Ten years ago? Why even five years ago . . .?'

He seemed a determined type and Shekar became a captive listener. The man was waiting for an answer still leaning his whole bulk to one side.

'No, I don't,' said Shekar.

'Ah, I thought so! One rupee per luggage of average size like your suitcase.' He waited for Shekar's reaction of astonishment. Shekar deliberately looked wooden.

This irritated the fellow. 'Now you generously pay five rupees! It is this kind of careless extravagance which is responsible for inflation . . . . '

Mercifully the guard's whistle simultaneously with a shrill hoot from the engine provided an escape for Shekar. The train began to move and the people on the platform floated away backward and disappeared, giving way to lampposts, stone buildings, signboards, railway hardware, slums, huts, factories and finally vast fields.

The fat fellow was now engrossed in a dog-eared book which seemed to be of a religious nature judging from the severe use it had evidently been subjected to and the red and yellow smudges on the faded jacket. Another passenger was checking the cash and papers in his oversized purse. Two others were engaged in conversation in secretive low tones, unaware, probably, of the fact that the train had started. Suddenly a strong flavour of fresh orange assailed Shekar. At the far end of the compartment a lady, who had the rough-and-ready look of one dedicated to things rural and their uplift, was peeling an orange.

In which part of the world could one come across such variety in such a limited space, Shekar mused! An article was germinating in his creative mind for *the Messenger.* But he felt depressed by the thought that probably by the time he returned *The Messenger* would be in the hands of a sugar merchant or a scrap iron dealer! He himself would be sitting at a table in an advertising agency writing copy to promote some pink soap '. . . it has the natural flavour of the freshness of forests in monsoon and contains the mineral oils of the earth to feed your complexion and keep it bright as dawn . . . .' From *The Messenger* his mind automatically jumped to Asha. The rendezvous with her the previous day at the Hotel Riviera's garden restaurant had pushed him rather too suddenly into a maze of plans, schemes, strategies which were all supposed to bring them together as man and wife and make them live happily ever after! Asha, of course, was in command of the situation and gave Shekar no chance to question her plan, the risk involved, the retribution to be faced at the hands of Sagar in case her strategy went awry. All the questions which came cropping up during their conversation were brushed aside by Asha as being minor details that would be tackled later. The more he listened to her the less hopeful he became of their ever getting married.

It seemed more certain he would end up in jail for abduction and rape. She would probably be married off to a sugar baron's son. He was torn between a great desire for her and the impossibility of consummating their union honourably as a wedded couple. Asha, for her part, was supremely confident and totally blind to the hazards of facing the volcanic fury of Sagar! Whenever he tried to bring this up she would ask, 'Are you getting scared?' 'Are you feeling nervous?' and laugh puckishly at him.

Shekar did not know if she was being serious in this matter or just playful. Her entire scheme seemed to be based on the romantic adventures of one of her classmates who, Shekar suspected, was the same one who had enlightened her about short-time room facilities provided at the Hotel Riviera.

According to Asha, there was a tiny temple in a patch of jungle on the outskirts of the city. In this temple there was an obliging priest. He was well versed in religious rituals and qualified to bring two souls together in holy wedlock. He would even secure the alliance with a temporary stamped certificate to protect the young ones from their parents and the police.

It was said he was once a flourishing lawyer. But he had renounced the world having become disgusted watching criminal minds at close quarters day after day. He had settled in this temple solving the problems of desperate souls. Asha was given to believe that the good priest helped out not less than fifty couples a month. Shekar began to accept the fact that Asha was talking in terms of a daring elopement one morning, getting married at the temple and disappearing to some remote place. It was as simple as that. Date and time of elopement, luggage to be carried, cash to be taken, transport to the temple and beyond were all minor details not to be bothered about at the garden restaurant of Hotel Riviera. Judged by Shekar's journalistic temper this copy seemed badly done, needing drastic editing and details for a proper conclusion. But Shekar let Asha ramble on without interruption and was content just to watch her lovely face and vivacious facial expressions. He fell for her all over again.

* * *

Shekar had not noticed during his reverie that the world outside had quietly darkened. An occasional spark of light from a lamppost fluttered past like an iridescent bird. The train had glided in and out of many wayside stations without his being aware of it. His fellow passengers had become subdued and were spreading their beds, folding their clothes and variously preparing to retire for the night.

Shekar had brought with him some sandwiches and a flask of coffee for dinner. He bit into a sandwich but it left a metallic taste in his mouth. As he was hungry and thirsty he had no choice but to carry on munching the sandwich and neutralizing the taste by gulping down coffee with each bite.

Then he climbed up to his reserved upper berth and stretched out on the bare rexine upholstery. He hoped he would go off to sleep cradled by the movement of the train. But his thoughts returned to Asha after a brief interval like in a cinema show. He began to analyse and assess her suggestions objectively and found them not so crazy after all. He admired her boldness: here she was an only daughter of a wealthy mafia don ready to sacrifice everything for Shekar's sake and face and defy her formidable father. It was stupid of him to expect in the matter of elopement a draft plan as if chalked out by a travel agency giving the details of date of departure, scheduled time, mode of transport, destination, room reservation and so on. It was left to the male of the species to sort all these out. First, he would look for a reliable taxi, fix a place for Asha to meet him. He wondered how big her suitcase would be and who would be carrying it to the meeting place. Surely he would not be churlish enough to let her carry it . . . she would have to squirrel out her things bit by little bit over the days and hide them away in a friend's place and later pack them in a box and . . . .

He fell fast asleep before he had charted out the elopement further.

The Cherry Choo-Choo

Victor Banerjee

THE 19TH OF MARCH 1927, would have been just another day if it were not the last day that the 'Cherry Choo-Choo' would stop at the little village station of Tangchik about forty miles north of Buksa Duar. It was also the day Jigme's Grandpa, Palden, picked to die.

It was in 1926, when Master Bridges (for he refused to be called Mister) twirled his handle-bar moustache and turned his sights to Taga Zong, beyond the Teesta valley, in the highlands along the banks of the Torsa, and decided to railroad the Sikkimese and immigrant Tibetans into a more civilized and British way of life.

Lumding in the north-east frontier was dangerous terrain and one of Bridges' colleagues, an engineer tunnelling through the Naga hills, had been devoured by a tiger whose widow bravely sat over the 'kill' and shot the beast. Bridges didn't pretend to be a hero, or an engineer, nor had he opted for a posting from Huddersfield to India to be devoured by a rabid rhinoceros in some backward tropical outback. He was of the ilk who hung a mosquito net like a visor under his solar hat and had natives beat the grass before he put a single foot forward, just in case he was stepping into a nest of mating cobras.

While Bridges sat back on his deck chair and smoked Nepalese tobacco in his briar pipe, the sun-burned natives had no idea what they were doing setting twin tracks of steel across the hills, high above the frothing white waters of the Teesta. Steam engines were still a novelty in England just like the puffing weed in Bridges' pipe that turned him red around the ears, gradually thrust his eyeballs out of their sockets until choking at death's door he would fly off his chair, cough his entrails out and bend right over on his knees till his wheezing curled the grass beneath his breath. He would then rise ashen-faced and not let the tobacco bother him till the bout next morning. The native labourers loved it and, during their break for salted raw tea, offered him some of their home grown stuff which Bridges always turned down with a sneer because they came out of grimy pockets mapped with salt licks of a fortnight's sweat and were proffered held between fingers that had travelled and explored who knows what, where.

Every evening just before sundown, little girls plucking tea on the slopes beyond Darjeeling would stop and giggle at a mad white man hurtling down the tracks on a trolley pedaled by red-turbaned Biharis whose bare knees below ill-fitted khaki shorts bristled with goose bumps, as the freezing mountain air swooped into their loins and flapped through their groin, across their bobbing bellies, under their chins and around and out past their collars. Bridges with his net sucked into his face and flapping like a pennant behind his stiff neck, looked like an azuri harem girl dashing to her annual appointment with the sheikh of Arabi.

Master Brides felt like a pioneer.

Often, while the trolley plummeted down hill, free-wheeling precariously around curves that lifted Bridges' scrotum into his tonsils, the Englishmen pondered upon writing his memoirs one day; but Huddersfield was a smog that he would never breathe again. Ironically, he would die three years later, of malaria, while studying French to marry the Missionary's daughter, in Chandanagore.

The steam engine arrived in Buksa Duar midst a standing ovation from the labourers of several plantations, who had gathered with their sahibs to gape at a wonder of the world.

The blue-eyed, brown-haired and pale-skinned Anglo-Indian engine driver who had rolled the 'Choo-Choo' into town, was whisked away by hordes of admirers, laced with rice wine that had fermented for weeks in diurnal anticipation of the arrival of the train and, in the morning, was discovered dead in a local brothel where, introduced as an Apollo from Calcutta, he succumbed to an endless striving to uphold his standard.

Master Bridges was lunching with the Chogyal of Yatang, savouring the idea of another British take-over, and sucking dripping noodles from his chin thrust above a bowl of *thukpa*, when news of the tragedy reached him. Out of respect for the Monarch, and in allegiance to stiff upper lips, he said not a word, though in keeping with the mysticism of the East, the sombre Chogyal was already aware of what had happened.

That is where the problems began, and where Jigme's grandfather, a jolly septuagenarian who refused to retire from active service, unexpectedly entered the scene heroically.

In a gravelly base voice tuned in the gumpas of ancient Tibetan monasteries the visionary Monarch said to Bridges, 'Tough.' Bridges nodded. His, future was at stake. Where in these God-forsaken mountains would he find an engine driver? 'Palden.' Bridges who hadn't spoken, wondered if the Monarch might have burped. 'Palden,' repeated the king. 'Pa-r-don?' queried Bridges, 'Palden' came the swift reply. 'Pardon?' 'Palden.' After the briefest of pauses, 'Pardonnez mois?' Tried Bridges, as a polite variant. 'Palden, my boiler room mechanic!' came an involuntary roar from a monarch whose tolerance was being tried. Bridges shrank behind a pile of steaming dumplings that had been set before him and asked most ingratiatingly, 'Why sir, what's he done? Aren't the dumplings to your Highness's liking?'

The Chogyal threw his head back and roared with laughter. With tears welling under both his slanted lids, he said, 'You English hardly ever learn to speak your own language. While we falter over your dialectic mispronunciations, your audacious presumption that we natives can never speak your King's English is terribly amusing. Palden, young man, could save your unpardonable neck and perhaps guarantee that your train leaves on its inaugural run to Taga Zong tomorrow. He is a genius with engines and with a few pointers might even save the day.' Bridges fell to his knees and, embarrassed and elated, kissed the hem of the Chogyal's brocade gown. If he could help it, Yatang would never be colonized.

That afternoon Jigme's grandpa, Palden, was whisked out of the boiler room of the summer palace in Gangtok and carried in a chair on the shoulders of porters, down to the plains of India, where a horse carriage transported him with Master Bridges to Buksa Duar. As they jolted down the country roads, Bridges opened up a manual that gave people in his rank a working knowledge of the knobs one twiddled and the chains one pulled to operate a steam engine. He turned to show it to the old man, but the tumble and sway of the carriage had turned Palden's yellowish face, green; his hill belly, bilious; the net result, motion sickness. Palden threw up.

When they arrived at the railway station, they were stopped by the funeral procession for Owen Bambridge, the engine driver. Master Bridges was expected and obliged to accompany the body of the dear deceased to the cemetery. Palden, still dizzy from the ride, looked sorrier than any one else in the congregation while everyone' hugged and consoled Master Bridges for the passing of 'Bam-Bridge,' who they presumed from the name, must have been a relative.

Lilies cast aside, Bridges took Palden to the engine parked at a siding, and there stared aghast at meters and brass knobs that hadn't featured in his obsolete catalogue. What could he say; Palden didn't speak a word of English though even he could recognize stupidity and ignorance in any face. Bridges began to feel nauseous and stepped down onto the tracks and squatted on the rails as he had seen his labourers do. The cold rail burned through his trousers like his old headmaster's cane. He had failed again.

With his head slumped between quaking knees, he heard a hiss. It was steam. The little engine gasped and gurgled and lurched forward in jerks and the wild grinning face of Palden appeared over the side as the locomotive gathered speed and began to run down the tracks until it suddenly lunged and raced in a cloud of smoke and steam towards the station. Palden looked out at Bridges who was running frantically alongside, screaming and yelling hysterically at Palden to pull the brake. Over the rattle and din of the engine, Palden, his every long, discoloured tooth visible in a maniacal grin, was screaming hilariously back at Bridges and never turned to look and see what was ahead.

Bridges receded and disappeared in clouds of dust and soot and as Palden stared, the passing station with women and children and the town's elders putting up streamers and banners for the next day's inauguration stopped their work to wave jubilantly at him: he scattered confetti in wind-blown eddying billows over everyone's head. Then suddenly, Palden was in open country. The breeze soothed and cooled his cheeks in the burning heat that blazed from the furnace he had stoked. It still had not dawned on Palden that he was alone, without any knowledge of how to stop or go back.

He pulled a chain, and the shinning whistle shrieked overhead. He pulled it again, and again; it shrieked and shrieked. He began enjoying this. He slowly moved a brass handle, and the needle on a meter above it moved too. He gave it a short yank and the air and cabin around him filled with steam. He cranked it back, and the engine gained speed. He moved another brass lever and the wheels began to squeak. He pulled and pulled, and it squeaked and squeaked. He gave it a turn, and was almost thrown into the red hot coals as the train slowed down.

Bridges meanwhile had mustered a trolley and was goading the poor Biharis to go faster and faster in pursuit. He could see the train in the distance. When he saw clouds of steam suddenly rise from it, he stood up on his seat, plugged his ears with his index fingers, and stared in horror; waiting for it all to blow up. When it didn't, he took off his solar *topee* and waved it in the air to set a rhythm for the poor Biharis who were breaking their backs for their crazed sahib.

Bridges couldn't believe his eyes when the trolley began to rapidly catch up with the train. Then to his utter consternation he realized that it was not his zeal that was propelling them faster, but old Palden's engine that was reversing full throttle towards them. He screamed at the Biharis to jam on the brakes and waited in shock for the skidding wheels to stop sliding on the tracks. With less than fifty yards to go he shouted, 'Abandon ship' and leapt off. The Biharis who had brought the trolley to a halt jumped off, threw the trolley off the rails and, just as they stepped aside, Palden steamed past waving and grinning at them.

At noon the following day, Bridges stood proudly beside Palden the engine driver as, midst the cheering of crowds and the wail of mismatched shehnais mixed with jungle drums and Buddhist chants, the little steam engine bedecked in marigolds pulled out of the station on its journey to Taga Zong. Bridges would always remain grateful to the native intelligence of the people of India.

It was on that historic journey, as they huffed and puffed past the drowsy village of Tangchik, where Palden originally came from, that Bridges promised to make a small station there, as a token of remembrance and gratitude. It was on that same dream journey that Palden and Bridges took the little train through some of the world's most spectacular scenery and cherry orchards.

Grandpa had told Jigme the story more than a hundred times. Each time the clusters of cherry blossom grew heavier on the boughs, and the flight of long-tailed blue magpies, golden orioles and scarlet minivets, painted special rainbows across their Himalayan skies; and each time a certain regret, and remorse, crept into the tale for having intruded upon, and tainted, paradise.

Grandfather Palden remembered how his brain had been lulled by the fragrant liquor he drank, and how his tired old knees shook while he danced with the beautiful women and children; how the people had welcomed the first supplies of salt, cotton from the mills of Bengal and English medicines they had never heard of before. When he left them, he returned with several hollowed bamboos filled with cherry brandy and a basket of cherry blossoms for Jigme. Ever since that first journey into the cherry blossom land, the train had been called the 'Cherry Choo-Choo'.

But the run proved unprofitable. The colonizers built no summer resorts, no traders arrived to set up shop in the poor little town of Tang Zong. In a couple of months, the authorities reduced the operation to just once a week, and now, after only a year, the service was being withdrawn altogether.

To the people of Tangchik it hardly made a difference. They lived happily in their sleepy mountain village and whenever the Cherry Choo-Choo passed, they would wave to it from their fields. It stopped at the little slate-roofed hut which was their station, and old Palden, who had been made the honorary station-master, would exchange a few words and a pink slip of paper with the driver who seldom stepped down. On the way back, the driver would hand Palden a long bamboo flask that would help the old man relive his visit to the paradise he once knew. Jigme and his friends from school always rushed to the station to greet the train and Jigme was always given pride of place on his granddad's knee while the old man told the class a little story about his adventures in Sikkim and, of course, Tang Zong. The village schoolmaster would spend the half hour staring at the little pink slip and sipping a small cup of cherry brandy that Palden agreed was fair recompense for letting the children chat with him one day, each week.

But the 19th of March was different. The entire village and all the schoolchildren had gathered at the station to bid farewell to their little toy wonder, the Cherry Choo-Choo. At around noon, little puffs of smoke appeared above the rolling hills, beyond the distant roofs of the last houses on the horizon. Old Palden was seated as usual with his feet up on the easy chair provided to him by the railways, fast asleep in the warmth of the glorious spring sunshine.

Then came the three short hoots, and that sweet little whistle that scared no one and made thrushes in scrubs stare in awe and wonder at God's genius; a shining metal bird with a long winding tail, descending flightless.

As the train turned a corner and came into sight, Master Bridges, the insane Englishman, could be seen standing on the roof waving madly with a bamboo in one hand and a garland of cherry blossoms in the other. The whistle kept blowing and engulfing Bridges in puffs of delicate steam. A wild cheer went up from the crowds who rushed onto the tracks and ran waving colourful scarves and sweaters towards the on-coming train. It was a wonder there was no accident that day as the train inched its way forward through a joyous wreath of waving bandanas and woollies who insisted on escorting her in.

As Bridges jumped to the ground, the crowd hoisted him on their shoulders and the Englishman looked like a frosted figurine on top of a meandering wedding cake as the people bore him to where Grandfather Palden, who had not risen from his chair, stared at the euphoric celebrations with the slightest of smiles creasing his wrinkled face. As Bridges was lowered to the ground and walked up to Palden swirling and swishing the cherry brandy in the bamboo flask, he sensed there was something wrong. Old Palden was dead.

Little Jigme often wondered if his Grandfather had died happy or sad. As his body was lowered into a shallow grave beside the blossoming mustard fields, the Cherry Choo-Choo's whistle blew its last plaintive farewell to Palden, the first master she had known. Bridges knelt down and placed the bamboo flask on the damp earth that now covered old Grandpa, and scattered the cherry blossoms over the top of his grave. Later, the Cherry Choo-Choo pulled away quietly, and the crowd that stood around it waved silently to Grandpa Palden's crazy English friend, Master Bridges.

The Eurasian engine driver turned to Bridges and asked, 'An old buddy?' 'No,' murmured Bridges with a sad smile, 'Half-devil and half-child, but by the living God that made him, he was a better man than I. A funny story; a wonderful memory.'

As the puffing iron-heart chugged beyond the ridge, little warm clouds of smoke dotted the horizon with a message only machines understood. A soft breeze blew gently, over a flask of cherry brandy and a mound of shimmering cherry blossoms.

The people of Tangchik never saw the Cherry Choo-Choo again.

99 UP

Manojit Mitra

THE NEWS SPREAD LIKE WILDFIRE, as any news did in Seulia. Ranjan Kumar was coming to town. The one and only Ranjan Kumar; the matinee idol of the Bengali screen; the face that beamed down at passers-by from a million walls. The Guru of all young men, the heart-throb of every girl that understood Bengali. He, himself, would be here.

No one quite knew how it started, but the news did the rounds swiftly, which was in character with sleepy little Seulia. So little ever happened here that any event, or the prospect of any event, was always big news and the story was passed on and lapped up eagerly by everyone. Have you heard . . . ? O yes, but of course, I knew it long before you did. Or O no, what is it, tell me for heaven's sake, is that so, my God, etc. and then the latest recipient shoots off to disgorge what he has just consumed. Most of the time, it was something about the daughter of so-and-so running away with so-and-so or someone having a fight with one's brother over property, or something of the kind. The people of Seulia had to make do with these stories because nothing of any earthshaking importance ever happened here.

Nor was any such thing on the cards. Seulia had no claim to distinction whatsoever. More than a hundred kilometers away from Calcutta, it was not quite a village, and had not yet made up its mind whether to grow into a town. It boasted two rice mills, one high school, a large number of grimy ponds that yielded no fish and a rickety cinema house with an asbestos roof. Thatched huts, pucca and semi-pucca houses stood shoulder to shoulder beside its dusty, cobbled roads. Cycle-rickshaws honked their horns. Bullock-carts trundled along. People walked slowly. The pace of life was slow as slow. No one in Seulia was ever in a hurry.

The one beautiful spot was the railway station. Located at the southern end of Seulia, it was small but picturesque. The station-master, known universally as master mashay, had a one-room office. The rest of the station was bare, with no godowns and waiting-rooms to spoil the view. From the platform, one could see undulating, open fields stretching into the horizon where stood the hazy, blue hills of Chhotanagpur. The landscape was dotted with Krishnachura, Radhachura and Palash trees. The station was hardly ever crowded. Barely half a dozen trains passed through Seulia throughout the day. Two of these were long-distance trains which thundered away haughtily, whistles blowing non-stop as if to ridicule the inconsequential little station. The others stopped, but for hardly a minute. The old men of Seulia often came to the station for their evening stroll. The young men, who had so little to amuse themselves with, would also came often and sit in groups and chat till late into the evening.

The master mashay lived in his small, brick-red quarters close by, but spent most of his time in his office and the platform, because he had nothing better to do. Nitai the mad man, Nitai Pagla to everyone, had no home at all and lived at the station. No one knew where he had come from and how he survived. Sometimes he sat at the same spot for hours. Then he would be galvanized into action all of a sudden. He would wave his hands, roll his eyes upwards and let out shouts of 'Hai! Hai! Huck! Harrrrrrr . . . .' and then charge away from the platform, down the tracks, towards the blue horizon. Some time later, he would, again, be seen sitting at one end of the platform, contemplating the tracks, lost to the world.

So what could bring the great Ranjan Kumar to such a pathetic little non-place? The story that emanated from Saha's tea shop, the birthhouse of many a tale, was that the big man would be here to attend the inaugural show of his latest film, *Naba Anuraag* (New Love), in Seulia talkies, the show-piece of the town and its only recreational centre, its only link with the world of dreams. Only old films ran here since the cinema had opened about five years ago, but for the first time, it owner, Manik Babu, the richest man of Seulia, had bagged a new film. *Naba Anuraag* would open here on Friday, along with show houses in Calcutta, which was a big step forward for the whole of Seulia and, to cap it all, Ranjan Kumar would attend the first show.

Initially, no one was quite sure, but as the story went round and round, and one heard it from more and more people, the uncertainty passed and it gained universal credence. What fuelled the gossip mill was Manik Babu's timely departure for Calcutta on Sunday. It was believed that he had gone there to escort Ranjan Kumar on his way to Seulia. There were one or two dissenting voices. At Saha's tea stall, Rajen Kundu, the local cynic, claimed that Manik Babu had actually gone to Calcutta to get stones removed from his gall-bladder. But everyone shouted him down. Several tea stall regulars said they had heard from the ushers and gatekeepers of the cinema that Manik Babu's mission was to bring Ranjan Kumar and that was that.

There was great excitement the next few days. It was taken for granted that Ranjan Kumar would arrive by the 99 UP from Calcutta. It reached Seulia at 2:30 in the afternoon, just in time for the first show at 3 o'clock. It was also agreed that everyone would be at the station in time to receive the big man. The girls, naturally, were most enthusiastic. In every house at Seulia, there were excited female voices discussing what they should on the big day. Many decided to carry garlands. In Kailash's hair-cutting saloon and Krishna hotel, Seulia football club and rice mills, all the talk was about Sunday and Ranjan Kumar. Coming to the station on Friday? Yes, of course. The secretary of the football club proposed a public reception for Ranjan Kumar, but others vetoed it, arguing that the big man would have no time to spare. Actually, they were more apprehensive of the way the secretary would go about it, being an irrepressible bungler.

In the high school, Sanskrit teacher Taranath Pandit tried to put the fear of God in the heart of every student. Film stars and their like should be ignored by students, he said, because they were filthy, immoral creatures. But in the staff room, he ran into heavy weather. The teachers of English and Mathematics called him prudish, ignorant and an antiquarian, living in the times of Manu. They had the impudence to suggest that he should chop off his pigtail and read film magazines! Taranath was livid.

Everyone, down to Matru the milkman and the rickshawallas, looked forward to the big day with great expectations. Spirits were generally high. Ignoring Taranath's warnings, the schoolboys visited Seulia talkies every day, where posters of *Naba Anuraag* were on display, the focal point being the beaming visage of handsome Ranjan Kumar. These visits boosted their spirits further. In every house, the girls giggled and repeated whatever they knew about his personal life, his loves and his marriages. Even the normally taciturn station-master was infected. A bachelor, he lived alone. He had no friends at Seulia to discuss such things with and was by nature a shy person. But in his heart, there was a soft corner for Ranjan Kumar. During his three years at Kharagpur station, he had seen several Ranjan Kumar films. He was in his mid-forties now, but in his heart of hearts, he liked to imagine himself as a dashing, romantic youth, much in demand among women, just like Ranjan Kumar on the silver screen. He did not participate in any discussion, but kept one ear cocked and quietly awaited his hero's arrival.

On Friday, small groups began to arrive at the station around noon. By 1 o'clock the up platform was jampacked. The late-comers spilled over to the down platform, grudgingly, because those on the up platform would be the first to see the star and would perhaps even be able to touch him. Everybody was there, except for Taranath Pandit who knew from the thin attendance in Class X that his campaign had failed. Girls stood in giggling, chattering groups, making mildly critical comments on the another's dress. The elderly women stood in a separate group. The young men jostled around jauntily. Loud pleasantries were exchanged. Even Rajen Kundu was there. His scepticism had gone down over the last few days, and looking at the large, expectant crowd, he also wanted to believe that he had been wrong. Many brought garlands for Ranjan Kumar. Matru the milkman was wearing a clean shirt, something no one had seen him doing for years. Inside the station office, the lonely station-master paced up and down, came out to look occasionally at the crowd, and retreated again into his room.

The only person who did not seem to enjoy the proceedings was Nitai Pagla. He was visibly irritated. Over the years, he had got used to being the lord of the station, where he could do as he pleased. He did not understand the sudden invasion of his privacy. Things turned worse when the school boys decided to amuse themselves by pulling his leg. After some time, he could take it no more. He gnashed his teeth, rolled his eyes heavenwards and broke into yells of 'Wheee . . . Hoa Hoa . . . Hiya hei . . . Harrrrr . . . .' Then he sprinted through the crowd and took off along his usual route down the tracks. This added to the general merriment. Some schoolboys pursued him for a little distance but Nitai was too fast for them. Soon he disappeared from view.

The tension became unbearable as the signal dipped. Only minutes to go before the great moment! Everyone jockeyed for a place on the edge of the platform and altercations broke out. There was much speculation about where the first class compartment would be located, and shouts of don't-step-on-my-toes. Some women complained shrilly that they were being pushed back. As the engine came into view, the crowd burst into thunderous applause.

Huffing and puffing, clanking and creaking, 99 UP entered Seulia station and came to a screechy halt. The lone first class compartment was last but one. As someone shouted, 'here', the entire crowd pushed in that direction. There was utter confusion. Only the strongest men could reach its two doors. Not many were likely to get off the first class anyway, for Seulia had few people who travelled first class. But one passenger did step out of it. It was Manik Babu, the cinema house owner.

There was another burst of applause. If Manik Babu was there, Ranjan Kumar was sure to follow. But there was no Ranjan Kumar. Manik Babu was quite flabbergasted at the wild reception. He wanted to know what was going on, but volleys of questions were fired at him before he could make himself heard. Where was Ranjan Kumar? Hadn't he come? Why? Would he come by the evening train? Was Ranjan Kumar ill? Would he come at all? So on and so forth.

It took Manik Babu several minutes to size up things. Then he patiently explained to the crowd that Ranjan Kumar was never expected, that he had not invited Ranjan Kumar, that he had gone to Calcutta for personal reasons. No, no, no, there were no stones in his gall-bladder. He had gone to attend his niece's wedding. There would be no opportunity to see Ranjan Kumar in flesh, but everyone was welcome to Seulia Talkies to see him at his best in *Naba Anuraag*. After buying tickets, of course. Heh Heh Heh. Then he strode away briskly. He had to be at Seulia Talkies on time for the first show.

The rear of 99 UP receded into the distance. As word went round, a hush fell on the platform. The crowd milled around, not quite able to grasp the tragedy. So Ranjan Kumar was never supposed to come? But everyone said he was coming? Not fair. Not fair at all. Come to think of it, Manik Babu should have invited Ranjan Kumar. It would have looked so grand. Who spread the story? Must have been those useless louts guzzling down tea at Saha's stall. What was the world coming to? Bad. Bad. Too bad.

Gradually, the disappointed crowd began to disperse. Some of the girls were on the verge of tears. The garlands were thrown away. Rajen Kundu tried to do an I-told-you-so but was promptly snubbed into silence by his friends. Matru the milkman muttered to himself as he walked home. The young men wanted to blame someone for the whole thing but could not decide on a target, which left them feeling even worse. The elderly women got into arguments among themselves. The station-master sat alone in his room, trying hard to read a novel. There were three more trains to pass. He came out of his office after half an hour. There was no one at the station.

On that evening, everything in Seulia seemed to have gone away. The schoolboys could not concentrate on their home tasks. The evening chat session at Saha's tea stall was desultory, and the participants left early for home. Even those who saw the first show of *Naba Anuraag* felt cheated, because they had hoped to see their hero in flesh and on the screen simultaneously. In every home, the women were dispirited.

The last train passed at 8.30. The station-master arranged his things and locked up his office. Now, to home and rest. The night guard would pick up the key from his quarters. The station-master stood on the platform and looked at the town. A few lights were on here and there, but they would go out soon. There was no electricity yet and Seulia went to bed early. It had nothing to amuse its people with till late in the evening. Well, this had promised to be a special day, but . . . . The station-master shivered. The wind blowing down from the distant hills was cold. The first touch of winter! October was only three days away. He must remember to bring his woollen muffler from tomorrow. The station-master slowly walked home.

The night wind kept blowing. It dragged away the flowers, papers and sundry other rubbish usually left behind by the crowd. The Krishnachura and Palash trees murmured softly, for a long time there was no other sound. Then there arose a full-throated cry, 'Ha Ha Ha Ha! Hoi Hai Huh! Huck Harrrrrr . . . .'